The Holocaust Camps

The Holocaust Remembered Series

The Holocaust Camps

Ann Byers

Enslow Publishers, Inc.

40 Industrial Road   PO Box 38
Box 398   Aldershot
Berkeley Heights, NJ 07922   Hants GU12 6BP
USA   UK
http://www.enslow.com

Library of Congress Cataloging-in-Publication Data

Byers, Ann.
    The Holocaust camps / Ann Byers.
        p. cm. — (The Holocaust remembered series)
    Includes bibliographical references.
    Summary: Describes the establishment of Nazi concentration camps
throughout Europe and their eventual use as a means of eliminating the Jews.
    ISBN 0-89490-995-9
    1. Holocaust, Jewish (1939–1945)—Juvenile literature. 2. World War,
1939–1945—Concentration camps—Juvenile literature. [1. World War,
1939–1945—Concentration camps.] I. Title. II. Series.
D804.34.B93 1998
940.53'18—dc21   97-37642
                                          CIP
                                          AC

Printed in the United States of America

10 9 8 7 6 5 4 3

Illustration Credits: United States Holocaust Memorial Museum, p. 9; Library of
Congress, courtesy of USHMM Photo Archives, p. 15; Bundesarchiv, courtesy of
USHMM Photo Archives, pp. 7, 18, 50; Arnold Bauer Barach, courtesy of USHMM
Photo Archives, p. 24; National Archives, Washington, D.C., courtesy of the
United States Holocaust Memorial Museum, pp. 13, 31, 35, 39, 64, 69, 91, 96, 100,
102, 105; Rijksinstituut voor Oorlogsdocumentatie, courtesy of USHMM Photo
Archives, pp. 33, 42; Created by Enslow Publishers, Inc., pp. 44, 53; Hadassah
Rosensaft, courtesy of the United States Holocaust Memorial Museum, p. 46;
Rosanne Bass Fulton, courtesy of USHMM Photo Archive, p. 50; Archives of
Mechanical Documentation, courtesy of USHMM Photo Archives, p. 56; Main
Commission for the Investigation of Nazi War Crimes, courtesy of USHMM Photo
Archives, pp. 48, 61, 75; Yad Vashem, Jerusalem, Israel, courtesy of the United
States Holocaust Memorial Museum, p. 61; National Museum of Auschwitz-
Birkenau, courtesy of USHMM Photo Archives, pp. 64, 72; Lorenz Schmuhl,
courtesy of USHMM Photo Archives, pp. 21, 77, 81; American Jewish Joint
Distribution Committee, courtesy of USHMM Photo Archives, p. 77; KZ
Gedenkstatte Dachau, courtesy of USHMM Photo Archives, p. 84; Harry Faiwl,
courtesy of USHMM Photo Archives, p. 96; David Wherry, courtesy of USHMM
Photo Archives, p. 96; Aviva Kempner, courtesy of USHMM Photo Archives, pp.
87, 99; Ann Byers, p. 108.

Cover Illustration: National Archives, courtesy of the USHMM (Nobel laureate
Elie Wiesel, who was sixteen years old in this photo, is the first person at far right
in the second bunk).

Contents

Introduction:

The Stage is Set

Like a cauldron of stew churning and bubbling over a flame, all of Europe seethed. The treaty that had ended World War I was supposed to bring peace—"eternal peace." However, Europe in the 1920s was anything but peaceful. No nation was at war with another, but old hatreds still boiled beneath the surface. Fear and distrust were everywhere. The issues that had led to war—nationalism, militarism, ethnic division, and a thirst for more land—were unresolved. The peace was fragile at best.

Far more threatening than the tensions among nations, however, was the unrest that simmered within each country, frequently erupting in riots. The war had left much of Europe devastated physically, economically, and emotionally. Roads, bridges, and train rails had been demolished; factories, shops, and homes were leveled. The wealth of nations had been spent on bombs and planes and other weapons of war that were now used and broken or worthless. Hospitals and cemeteries throughout Europe were full. The people and their land were shattered.

Nowhere was the situation more stark than in Germany. Nearly three million of the country's sons and fathers had been killed or were missing in a war they had lost. Portions of German territory had been stripped away by the terms of the peace treaty, and the size of the army had been drastically reduced. Germany was no longer allowed to have an air force at all. And the victors had demanded that Germany accept all the blame for the war and pay reparations (payment to every country for all the damages the war had caused). The German people felt humiliated and angry.

In order to finance its recovery and pay its debts, the German government printed money, even though Germany had nothing to give that money value. Before the war, 4.2 German marks could be exchanged for one dollar. But by the end of 1923, it took 4.2 *trillion* marks to equal a dollar. People carried their money in wheelbarrows. Barely ten years after the war ended, when Germany, like every other nation, was struggling to rebuild its cities, its economy, and its spirit, the crash of the American stock market plunged the entire world into the Great Depression. Almost overnight, prices soared and earnings plummeted. Companies went out of business and stores closed their doors. In 1932, 6 million Germans were out of work—40 percent of the total labor force. (By comparison, unemployment in other European countries averaged 25 percent.)

In 1933, when Germany was looking for a savior from its turmoil, Adolf Hitler became chancellor of the country. On opposite page, Hitler reviews thirty-five thousand troops who came to Berlin to celebrate the third anniversary of his chancellorship.

The turmoil that frayed the country was a breeding ground for political and civil discontent. In the last days of the war, the kaiser (Germany's ruler) had fled the country and the leaders who were left, in panic and confusion, established the Weimar Republic to conduct the business of government. A citizenry that had lived for centuries under the dictatorship of an emperor struggled to learn how democracy worked. Communists, who wanted the common people to overthrow their leaders, incited demonstrations at every opportunity. Fascists, who wanted all power concentrated in a strong central government, also staged riots.

Into this fractured, demoralized, angry Germany of the 1920s and 1930s came Adolf Hitler. The son of an Austrian government worker and a peasant girl, this high-school dropout had climbed his way to the top of the extremist National Socialist German Workers' (Nazi) party. As its leader, Hitler had total control over the party and its fifteen-thousand-member private police force. He set about expanding his influence.

In huge, open-air rallies, he spoke to the defeated masses about German honor. He whipped young crowds into a frenzied enthusiasm when he exalted Germany's military tradition. He enthralled thousands at a time with his appeal to national pride. Hitler gave the people a cause around which to unite: the supremacy of the Aryan race (people of Germanic ancestry). He gave them a rallying cry for the restoration of Germany's greatness: Germany for Germans. And he gave them a focus on which to vent all their anger and lay all their blame: the Jews.

In his speeches, Hitler laid the total responsibility for World War I on the Jews. The Jews, he claimed, controlled Germany's finances and manipulated the press. He accused the Jews of conspiring with the Communists of Russia to start worldwide revolutions. Their goal, he warned, was to completely dominate every nation on earth.

Hitler's denunciation of Jews was not merely a tool for getting his party elected and for uniting the people. It was a personal passion. When he became chancellor of Germany (the leader of the country) in 1933, his anti-Semitism (hatred of Jews) became national policy. Within ten weeks, Germany enacted the first of 664 laws that deprived Jews of their citizenship, their rights, their dignity, and, ultimately, their very lives. Six years later, when he plunged his country into the largest and most costly conflict the world had known, he exploited Jews fiendishly. He used Jewish labor to build the weapons of war, he starved Jewish families to feed his armies, and he used the fervor of battle to make the murder of Jews a civic duty.

So strong was Hitler's determination to destroy all Jews that, even when German troops were beginning to lose ground on the battlefields of Europe and Russia, trains that were desperately needed to carry supplies and reinforcements were instead assigned to transport Jews to their deaths. Hitler's last recorded words, written on the day before he took his life, when he knew the war was lost, called the leaders and citizenry of Germany to "merciless opposition" to the Jewish people.

This attempt to completely annihilate an entire group of people has become known as the Holocaust. It nearly succeeded. In the twelve years that Hitler ruled Germany, from 1933 until his suicide in 1945, approximately six million Jews were killed. Two thirds of the Jews of Europe were wiped out—90 percent of all the Jews living in Germany and Poland. Some died from deliberate starvation and maltreatment in the cities. Others were executed by armed death squads created solely for the purpose of murder. The greatest numbers perished in the concentration camps.

11

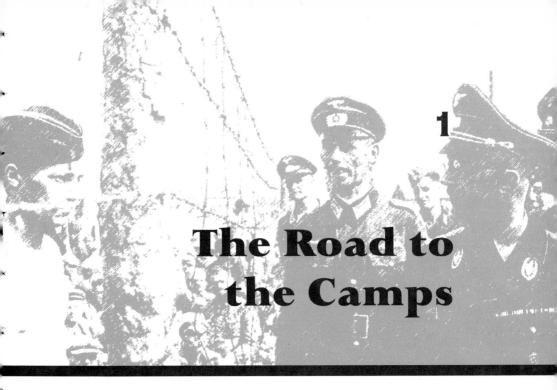

1

The Road to the Camps

Although unimaginable to a rational mind, a system of hundreds of camps used for isolating, torturing, and murdering men, women, and children was the natural conclusion of Adolf Hitler's twisted logic. Hitler had adopted a philosophy common in the 1920s: that Jews were inferior and evil. In his autobiography, *Mein Kampf*, written during the year (1923–24) he spent in prison beginning at age thirty-four, Hitler traced his feelings of revulsion for Jews to his early twenties. After merely observing Jews, he developed a disdain for them. "I began to hate them," he wrote of the Jews he saw at that time. "I became an anti-Semite."[1] In his hatred, Hitler considered all Jews unclean, subhuman, like maggots in a rotting body. It was reasonable to him that decent society should be scrubbed clean of such filth.

Anti-Semitism is closely linked with another philosophy Hitler championed: the supremacy of the Aryan race. Hitler believed that German culture embodied the highest forms of art and learning. He saw the tall, blond, blue-eyed Aryan as superior to any other race of people. Black-haired Jews who followed their own traditions were blights on this glorious culture and threats to the purity of this "master race." It followed naturally to Hitler that, for the good of the German people, Jews must be eliminated.

Years before he came to power, before he wrote *Mein Kampf*, Hitler had penned a letter spelling out clearly the obvious end to his determined pursuit of anti-Semitism: "Its final objective must unswervingly be the removal of the Jews altogether."[2]

Hitler's unashamed personal campaign against the Jews laid the foundation upon which the concentration camps were later erected. Many obstacles, however, stood in the way of making the grotesque concept a reality. Germany was governed by laws that would never permit such a thing. Those laws would have to be changed. People would be outraged at gross mistreatment of their neighbors. They would have to be desensitized. Resistance was certain to occur; some would refuse to go along with the program. They would have to be brought in line by force.

Legal Basis

When he became chancellor on January 30, 1933, Hitler immediately began the process that would

A plate from Alfred Vogel's text Erblehre und Rassenkunde in Bildicher Darstellung, *which juxtaposed the faces of German and Jewish children for racial classification. The Jewish children were forced to live in ghettos and concentration camps while the non-Jewish children were encouraged to commit anti-Semitic acts.*

Deutſche Jugend   Jüdiſche Jugend

14jähriger deutſcher Junge   14jähriger deutſcher Junge   14jähriger Judenjunge[1]   13jähriger Judenjunge

13jähriges deutſches Mädchen   8jähriges deutſches Mädchen   8jähriges Judenmädchen   14jähriges Judenmädchen[1]

7jähriger deutſcher Junge   7jähriger Judenjunge

Aus dem Geſicht ſpricht die Seele der Raſſe

[1] Aus „Die Judenfrage im Unterricht" von Finkh. Stürmer-Verlag, Nürnberg

eventually result in the creation of a network of over one thousand concentration camps.

The first step in building the concentration camps was the establishment of a legal basis for acts of the most brutal inhumanity. Through a combination of political maneuvering, scare tactics, and bullying, Hitler was able to suppress all voices but those of the Nazi party and to neutralize all authority but his own. Less than two months after he took office, he succeeded in pushing through the legislature the Law for Removing the Distress of People and Reich. It became known as the Enabling Act because it enabled Hitler to do whatever he pleased.

This law gave Hitler, as chancellor, the power to suspend the constitution he had sworn to protect. It allowed him to make laws without the approval of any other person or group—laws that could be completely contrary to those he had taken an oath to uphold. The Enabling Act permitted him to disregard all appointed and elected officials, including the president. By this single act, Adolf Hitler had become, quite legally, the absolute dictator of Germany. Now anything he wanted could become the law of the land.

Hitler used this power to put the second brick in the wall of the concentration camps: the dehumanization of the Jewish people. He proclaimed a series of laws that tore their rights from them one by one. First, Jews were not allowed to hold government offices or to work as lawyers, jurors, or judges. Then they were disqualified from serving as doctors or dentists in government institutions. The number of Jews who could attend schools and colleges was drastically reduced, and no Jew was permitted to teach in a public school. One law barred Jews from the arts and entertainment; another kept them from working at newspapers. The Nuremberg Laws of 1935, named after the city in which they were announced, denied citizenship to Jews and forbade Jews to marry German citizens.

Anti-Semitism

The legal isolation and degradation of the Jewish people were reinforced by anti-Semitic publications. Newspapers attacked Jews with articles that declared, "The Jews are our downfall!"[3] Brightly colored posters screamed wild accusations and denounced Jews as "enzymes of destruction" and "racial tuberculosis."[4] Germany in the 1930s was deeply anti-Semitic. Thus, as the Jews were rapidly losing their rights as citizens and as human beings, their neighbors, for the most part, believed that they were getting only what they deserved.

Brutality

The final step in the construction of the concentration camp system was the use of brutality to terrorize the people into submission.

Long before coming to public office, Hitler, as leader of the Nazi party, had his own police force. In 1933, this private army boasted four hundred thousand men— four times more than the number of soldiers the entire country of Germany was allowed under the terms of the World War I peace treaty.[5] Hitler's Nazi soldiers were called the *Sturmabteilung* (SA) or Storm Troops and, because of the color of their uniforms, came to be known as the Brown Shirts. These fanatical young men, who pledged their loyalty not to Germany but to Hitler, roamed the streets of cities throughout the country, bent on violence. SA squads arrested and beat people at the slightest provocation. They taunted crowds into rioting against Jewish shopkeepers and damaging Jewish property. In the city of Nuremberg alone, over two hundred incidents were recorded between 1922 and 1933 of the desecration of Jewish graves.[6]

17

Since Jews had been made the number one enemy of the state, the growing brutality against them was not punished. In fact, Hitler encouraged it. Even before he took over the reins of government, he admitted proudly that he planned to increase the level of savagery in the forces he commanded:

> We must be ruthless. . . . Terror is the most effective political instrument. . . . It is my duty to make use of every means of training the German people to cruelty. . . . A violently active, dominating, intrepid, brutal youth—that is what I am after.[7]

The four hundred thousand Brown Shirts were not brutal enough for Hitler. From their ranks, he selected the most dependable and the most disciplined and molded them into a special bodyguard for himself and other Nazi leaders. This elite unit of Black Shirts became known as the *Schutzstaffel*, or SS. At first, it was a small band of 280 dedicated loyalists. But its leader, Heinrich Himmler, recruited tens of thousands of fanatical, anti-Semitic Nazis until he had created a military-style police force that was fiercer than the Storm Troops and much more willing to submit to Hitler's orders. Eventually, in June 1934, Hitler relieved the head of the SA, Ernst Roehm, of his duties and ended his life in a bloody purge. The Black Guard (SS) soon replaced the Brown Shirts as the primary instrument of terror. Together with the Gestapo (*Geheime Staatspolizei*, the State Secret

An elite unit known as the Schutzstaffel, *or SS, was set up by Hitler as a primary instrument of terror. The SS was Hitler's personal guard unit and its members served as executioners in concentration camps. In this picture, a regular police officer (on left) walks on the streets of Berlin with an SS auxiliary policeman.*

Police), the SS formed the capstone in the building of the concentration camps.

The camps were the tools whereby nearly all of the Jewish population of Europe was systematically humiliated, then tortured, and finally executed. The unspeakable atrocities of the concentration camps do not represent an evolution of Hitler's personal disdain for Jews; they were his desire from the beginning. In a 1920 speech, Hitler promised his audience to "carry on the struggle until the last Jew is removed from the German Reich."[8] *Mein Kampf* called for the killing of thousands of Jews by poison gas. Hitler's message to the Nazi party at a meeting in 1922 was unmistakable: "There can be no compromise—there are only two possibilities: either victory of the Aryan or annihilation of the Aryan and the victory of the Jew."[9]

And so he carefully and methodically set up the structures through which his aim could be achieved and created an atmosphere that made it not merely possible, but expected. He manipulated the government until he had the legal sanction to commit acts contrary to the laws of nature and of the state. He harangued the people until he had convinced many that Jews were bloodsucking parasites who did not deserve to live. He perfected a reign of terror until very few were willing or able to resist.

The network of concentration camps, which was to become the primary instrument of Hitler's campaign against the Jews, was developed less methodically. First, prison camps were established to detain and punish any who threatened the peace. Then, as World War II destroyed men and materials, forced labor camps provided Jewish workers to build the machinery for war. Finally, as all opposition was eliminated and the public conscience dulled, camps were built for the "final solution" of the Jewish problem: mass extermination.

2

The Prison Camps

T he first concentration camps were not built for Jews. In fact, the first ones were not even planned. They sprang up out of political necessity.

Before Hitler could begin to translate his anti-Semitism into national policy, he had to consolidate his power and remove all opposition. He could not allow other groups to do what his Nazis had done: bully their way to the top. He had to eliminate any threat to his absolute leadership. The Communists were the greatest danger. They had succeeded in toppling a regime that had ruled Russia for four hundred years and seemed bent on overthrowing every other government in Europe. The Social Democrats were a close second because they opposed Hitler and his policies. Other democratic parties and a Catholic party also had some popular support. They all had to be broken if Hitler was to govern uncontested.

Hitler accused his enemies of endangering the security of the country and had them arrested. The Storm Troops, the private army of the Nazi party; the SS, Hitler's elite guard; and police forces of various localities dutifully took into custody hundreds of people who were labeled threats to the state. Many of the Brown Shirts, who enjoyed the power their guns and uniforms gave them, took advantage of their positions and the atmosphere of chaos. They stopped people at random, beat them to satisfy their lust for violence, and held them for ransom.

All the jails in Germany did not have enough room to hold the thousands Hitler considered his opposition and the hundreds who were caught with them in the web of oppression. So empty factories and fortresses were hurriedly converted into temporary detention facilities.

On March 20, 1933, three days before the Enabling Act was passed, Heinrich Himmler, chief of police for the city of Munich, announced to the press that he was transforming an unused munitions plant—a gunpowder factory—ten miles northwest of Munich into a camp where "all Communists and, where necessary, [other officials] . . . who endanger state security are to be concentrated."[1] The next day, two hundred Communist prisoners were brought to the camp. Thus, on March 22, the day before the Enabling Act officially gave Hitler the legal sanction to crush anyone he disliked in any way he wanted, the first concentration camp was in operation outside the city of Dachau.

"Protective Custody"

The early arrivals to Dachau were not criminals; they were political opponents of Hitler. Technically, they had not been arrested; they had been placed in "protective custody." Protective custody was a police measure used not to shield citizens from harm but to "protect the State against subversive activity." It could be applied to "persons whose behavior endangers the existence and security of the people and State."[2]

The first inmates of Dachau were Hitler's political opponents: Communists, Socialists and other democrats, and political Catholics.

Dachau was built with twenty barracks, each made to hold 250 men—a total of 5,000. It was not designed to punish criminals. It was built so that the Nazi regime could flex its muscle and intimidate its foes. Its purpose was political control and its method was terror.

Conditions were harsh and treatment was brutal. Rows of wooden planks served as beds in barracks that were damp and without light or heat. Rations of food were meager. Prisoners were made to stand for hours at a time, burned with lighted cigarettes, beaten with clubs and wet towels, and flogged with wire-bound whips.[3] When they were released, their true accounts of life in Dachau were enough to spread the fear that was Hitler's primary instrument of power.

By the end of Hitler's first week of total control of Germany, fifteen thousand people were in protective custody.[4] Six months later, the concentration camps held twenty-seven thousand political prisoners. During his first tumultuous year, eighty thousand to one hundred thousand "dangerous" people had been detained, although seldom were more than twenty-seven thousand interned at any given time.

The sheer number of political prisoners necessitated more and more detention centers. In the first few months of 1933, forty to fifty improvised camps dotted the country. Each camp operated independently. This haphazard arrangement would not last long in a regime that prided itself on order and efficiency. Himmler worked to make Dachau a model—*the*

The camps were structured so that escape from them was nearly impossible. From a watchtower, guards could see the prisoners behind the electrified fence that surrounded the camp in Dachau.

model—for all others. He appointed Theodor Eicke commandant.

Camp Order

Eicke immediately began to formulate a list of regulations for maintaining "discipline and order." For infractions ranging from making a "jeering remark" to inciting rebellion and attempting to escape, inmates were to be punished by eight to forty-two days additional detention, hard labor, solitary confinement, twenty-five lashes with a whip, or death. Depending on the offense, death would be by shooting or hanging.[5]

Guards took an oath to enforce the disciplinary code "ruthlessly and without mercy."[6]

Immediately after Eicke drafted his rules, Himmler shut down several of the smaller concentration camps, releasing many of their inmates and moving others to larger camps. By the summer of 1937, all the makeshift facilities were closed and their seven to eight thousand prisoners sent to one of four camps: Dachau in the south, Sachsenhausen in the north, Buchenwald in between, and Lichtenburg for women. The Dachau regulations for treatment of inmates became standard practice in all the camps.

Eicke also developed a code of conduct and a training regimen for camp guards. The soldiers who patrolled and operated the camps became known as *Totenkopfverbände*—Death's Head detachments. They wore on their uniforms the skull and crossbones insignia that was their namesake. Men who would become commandants of later concentration camps learned how to intimidate, torture, and kill at Dachau.

From the beginning, the lords of this model camp established control through barbarity and maintained order through fear. No challenge or affront, no matter how slight, went unpunished. Three weeks after the first internees arrived, four tried to cross the electrified barbed-wire fence and the moat that surrounded the compound. The guns of the guards mowed down three and seriously injured the fourth. A month later, two townspeople were arrested and held until morning for merely attempting to peer over the wall to see what the inside of the camp was like. The newspapers published a warning from the Supreme SA Command that any such curious people would "be given the opportunity of studying the camp from inside for longer than just one night."[7]

Early Deaths

It was easy for the camp administration to justify the shootings of escapees. It was not hard to rationalize the executions of prisoners who violated camp rules, even though the regulations mandated death for fairly minor offenses. But the deaths of inmates from the sadism of the guards was more difficult to explain to those outside. One of the first such incidents recorded at Dachau took place the night of May 25, 1933, barely two months after the camp opened.

The Nazis were meticulous about record keeping, so the death of Sebastian Nefzger was reported to the Dachau County Court, as was the custom for all deaths in the court's jurisdiction. The accompanying summary of the camp doctor's postmortem examination claimed that Nefzger took his own life: "Death was not due to any external influence. There exists no doubt that death was due to bleeding from a cut in the artery of the left wrist."[8]

The chief public prosecutor, however, disagreed. A coroner's investigation ruled out suicide and established that the thirty-year-old political prisoner was strangled to death.

That same month another inmate, Leonhard Hausmann, was shot because, according to the guard, he was attempting to escape while on a work detail near the camp and refused to comply with the guard's order to halt. But the prosecutor learned that the bullet had entered Hausmann from a distance of less than twelve inches.

The number of violent deaths began to mount and the inconsistencies between official explanations and the coroner's findings continued. The chief public prosecutor filed criminal charges against individual camp guards, the camp doctor, and camp officials. He began an investigation and elicited Himmler's promise of full cooperation.

But Himmler's authority, as a high-ranking Nazi, was above the law. The prosecutor received a directive from his superior ordering him to discontinue the investigative proceedings because they would be "detrimental to the image of the National Socialistic State."[9] And so the only rein on the Death's Heads' savagery was the whim of the camp commandant.

Addition of Asocials

Toward the end of 1936 a new use was found for the concentration camps. Hitler was preparing Germany for the war he had already decided to launch. He had begun his Four-Year Plan for building a military machine that would restore German honor and give the Aryan people the *Lebensraum*—the living space—he felt they deserved. Hitler had long believed—and had written in *Mein Kampf*—that Germany was entitled to expand its borders to fill the land to the east (Poland and Russia). Acquiring *Lebensraum* meant war, and war required preparation. Weapons and equipment had to be built, food had to be grown and stored, new forms of fuel had to be created. Laborers were needed. But the push for rearmament had already put most of the country back to full employment, so workers were difficult to find. The concentration camps, however, held at any one time thousands of unproductive men, fully able to work.

In addition, the Nazis scoured Germany for others they could exploit for their work projects. They rounded up criminals and people they called asocials—those who were not in the mainstream of society—and brought them to the concentration camps. These were people who were not contributing to society: vagrants, beggars, drunkards. Eventually, gypsies and followers of various religious groups were also included. The government could make them useful. Unlike the political prisoners, these were destined to be permanent residents of the camps.

The next two concentration camps, patterned after Dachau, were still primarily detention facilities. But they were located in areas where captive labor could best serve the Reich. Sachsenhausen, which opened in August 1936, was close to Berlin, the capital. Buchenwald began operation in July 1937 near the Krupps armament works, which manufactured ammunition, guns, and tanks. Although these camps provided a much needed labor pool, this was not their primary function in the early years. Their main purpose was still to house political opponents for long enough to break their resistance to the Nazi government and to instill fear in others who might be similarly inclined.

With the exception of the criminals and the asocials, prisoners were detained for limited periods of time and then let go. After the release of many who had been apprehended in the initial internment of dissidents in 1933, the population of all the camps stayed around seven to eight thousand until 1938.

More Camps

A series of events in 1938 and 1939 swelled the ranks of the concentration camps. The first was Hitler's annexation of neighboring lands: Austria, which had been a part of the German empire until World War I, and the Sudetenland of Czechoslovakia, which contained 3 million Germans. Then Hitler raised the German flag over the Czechoslovakian provinces of Bohemia and Moravia. These were, for the most part, bloodless takeovers—not actual war yet . . . merely its prelude.

With each conquest, new arrests were made. Mobile "action groups," called the *Einsatzgruppen*, followed the soldiers, ferreting out political enemies in the newly acquired lands. Additional facilities were needed to accommodate the growing prisoner population. Dachau was enlarged—the inmates themselves constructed the barracks—and two new camps were built. Mauthausen was erected in Austria immediately after that country fell, and Flossenbürg was built in the mountains of Germany. The camps were located near stone quarries so that the prisoners could dig out the granite for the building projects of the Reich. Mauthausen was barely finished before the first nine hundred prisoners were interned.

Pressure on Jews

Although anti-Semitism was more rampant than ever and Jews were persecuted relentlessly and legally, the concentration camps still contained relatively few Jews. The thrust of Hitler's campaign against the Jews was not to imprison them, but to make their lives so miserable that they would leave the country of their own accord. His plan was to see Germany *Judenrein*, Jew free. Indeed, from the time the Nazis came to power until 1938, about 22,500 Jews fled from Germany each year. But the majority remained. They were slow to leave the people and places that had been "home" for generations. Many believed the nightmare of persecution must soon come to an end.

But the addition of Austria and the Czechoslovakian provinces to the Reich brought with it well over 350,000 more Jews. Some were the very people who had escaped from Nazi oppression in Germany just months earlier. Official pressuring of Jews to move elsewhere intensified. Jews were banned from many types of jobs. A large number had their property confiscated. In some places, they were barred from entering all businesses, including grocery stores; they could not buy milk or meat or medicines. Random harassment occurred in city after city. Synagogues—Jewish houses of worship— were desecrated, set on fire, or torn to the ground. And still, all the Jews did not leave.

So the government made Jewish emigration easier. It issued exit permits liberally. It sent trucks to carry people and their possessions to the east. It arrested wealthy Jews and took their money to pay for the transport of poor ones. Although Jews in the newly annexed territories fled by the thousands, a large Jewish community remained in Germany. More pressure needed to be applied to its members.

An excuse for that pressure came in November 1938. A seventeen-year-old Jewish refugee assassinated a minor official at the German embassy in Paris, France. Two nights later, demonstrations erupted throughout Germany. Reported as spontaneous reactions of the people to the assassination, the rampage was actually carefully organized by high-ranking leaders of Hitler's Security Service, SS, and Gestapo.

From one o'clock in the morning of November 10 until evening that day, German citizens set fire to 191 synagogues, 171 Jewish houses and apartments, and other buildings. They smashed the windows of seven thousand Jewish-owned stores and carried their contents to their own homes. They killed at least ninety-one Jews and seriously injured another thirty-six. This calculated orgy of vandalism and mayhem became known as *Kristallnacht* (Crystal Night)—the Night of Broken Glass.

At the end of the murderous spree, thirty thousand Jews had been arrested in several cities. They were taken to the concentration camps of Dachau, Buchenwald, and Sachsenhausen. An additional sixty-five hundred

Germans pass by the broken window of a Jewish-owned business that was destroyed during Kristallnacht. *This shop was one of seven thousand businesses that were smashed and looted. After this tragic event, thirty thousand Jews were placed under arrest and sent to concentration camps.*

were taken into "protective custody" in Vienna, Austria, and sent to Dachau and Mauthausen. Most were held for only a few weeks. The plan was not to punish the Jews—except economically—for the destruction orchestrated by the Nazi officials. The plan was to convince all Jews in the Reich, through fear, that they would be better off elsewhere.

The intimidation worked. In 1939, sixty-eight thousand Jews fled Germany and its occupied territories, almost twice as many as the previous year.

31

But they soon found themselves back under the iron fist of the Reich. On September 1, 1939, Hitler invaded Poland, beginning World War II. For three years, the German armies gobbled up one country after another: Denmark, Norway, Holland, Belgium, Luxembourg, France, Yugoslavia, Greece. By June 1941, the conquest stretched all the way to the borders of Russia.

With each German victory, the population of the concentration camps grew. New camps were built: Stutthof in Danzig, Auschwitz in Poland for Polish prisoners, Danica first and then others in Croatia, and Natzweiler with its twenty satellite camps in France. For the most part, however, the new internees, like the original inmates, were not Jewish. Hitler's temporary solution to the "Jewish problem" was to deport Jews farther and farther east. And when he ran out of places to put them, he herded them into crowded sections of cities called ghettos, walled the ghettos off, and kept them captive there. The concentration camps, in the summer of 1941, were still prisons not for Jews, but for political opponents and foreign prisoners of war.

By winter, however, the fortunes of war had changed. With the shift came a drastic change in the purpose, the population, and the operation of the camps.

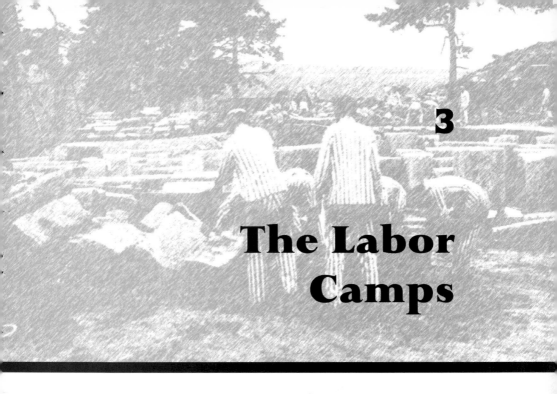

The Labor Camps

Hitler's invasion of Russia in June 1941 was a turning point in the war and for the concentration camps. Until then, every conquest had been easy and quick. The German *blitzkrieg*— lightning war—had stunned country after country and complete victory seemed within easy grasp. But the Russian campaign was unexpectedly long and difficult. Unpaved roads, subzero temperatures, and fierce resistance mired the German Army in a losing offensive. Coupled with the British refusal to surrender in the west, the standstill with Russia in the east forced Germany into a two-front war. By winter, military strategists had abandoned their hope of an easy end to the conflict. Instead of blitzkrieg, they settled in for a war of endurance.

A long, drawn-out war meant using more tanks, more planes, more bombs. It meant finding ways for an already overworked populace to produce even more armaments. It meant conscripting the workers of the weapons factories into the army and finding new laborers to replace them. One ready source of labor was the concentration camp. As Germany continued to expand to the east, truckload after truckload of war prisoners from Poland and Russia were emptied into the camps. The concentration camps could accommodate an inexhaustible supply of potential workers.

By the winter of 1941–42, the camps housed one hundred thousand inmates, most foreign casualties of war. Six major camps were each ringed by a dozen or more satellite camps—smaller, nearby operations that were built to increase the capacity of the camp system and provide additional work sites. Additional facilities were under construction or in the planning stages. The camps were deliberately transformed from detention centers to slave-labor operations. Their primary purpose was no longer political, but economic. General Oswald Pohl, chief of the SS Central Economic and Administrative Office, described the shift necessitated by the disastrous Russian campaign:

> The war has brought a manifest change in the structure of the concentration camps along with a fundamental change in their mission. . . . The detention of prisoners for reasons of security, correction, and prevention is no longer the first priority. The center of gravity has shifted to the economic side. The mobilization of the labor power of all internees primarily for war tasks (increase of armaments) must take absolute precedence.[1]

The ill-fated offensive against Russia also marked a turning point for the Jews. Germany's military strategists had expected Russia to fall as easily as her neighbors, but instead the campaign dragged on miserably and the German generals tasted their first major defeat. Hitler spewed the venom of his frustration on the foe that he was confident he could defeat: the

Jews were not the first prisoners of the concentration camps. The Nazis also rounded up political enemies, usually Communists, and placed them into the camps. Above, Heinrich Himmler speaks to a young Soviet prisoner during an official visit to a POW camp.

Jewish people. He blamed "the Jew" for instigating the war and for keeping it going. He ranted against the Jew as the "enemy of humanity" and accused Judaism of trying to "destroy the world."[2] On January 20, 1942, with the German Army in retreat from Moscow, top officials from Germany and its allies met to determine the fate of the Reich's 11 million Jews.

The Wannsee Conference

The conference was held in Wannsee, a suburb of Berlin. Two of the major figures there were Reinhard

Heydrich, head of security for the entire Reich, and Adolf Eichmann, chief of the SS Department of Jewish Affairs. Heydrich was ruthless in his treatment of everyone the Nazis considered enemies. He was called the Blond Beast and the Man with an Iron Heart. Eichmann was in charge of all the details of transportation for the emigration and deportation of Jews. He later boasted that he would leap into his grave laughing because he had a part in the deaths of millions of Jews. These two men and others like them were given the assignment of coming up with a comprehensive plan to keep the Jews from ever troubling Germany again. These men were to devise a "final solution" to the Jewish question.

Before the Russian campaign, Germany's policy regarding Jews had been forcible evacuation to Poland, where they were cruelly mistreated. Thousands had died from the inhumane conditions of the journey, starvation and brutality in the ghettos, and outright execution for spurious offenses. In its first year, thirteen hundred people starved to death in Warsaw, just one of twenty-four Jewish ghettos.

With the invasion of Russia, a new solution began to appear among the action groups—the *Einsatzgruppen*. These were not military battalions but political forces that accompanied the army in the early, victorious stages, apprehending political enemies. In Russia, however, spurred by their own anti-Semitism and the blood-lust of their commanders, these groups became roving death squads, rounding up Jews as well as Russian officials, and gunning them down by the thousands. The leader of one of the four *Einsatzgruppen* units estimated that his force alone massacred ninety thousand Jewish men, women, and children in a single year.[3] Thus, Nazi policy regarding Jews was emigration, but Nazi practice was brutality and murder.

The Wannsee Conference formalized practice into policy. The final solution to the Jewish question, as recorded in the minutes of the meeting, was to subject Jews to forced labor and work them to death:

> In big labor gangs with separation of sexes, the Jews who are capable of work are brought to these areas (in the Eastern occupied territories) and employed in road building, in which task undoubtedly a large part will fall out through natural diminution [that is, death].[4]

Those who survived the rigorous slave labor were to be accorded "appropriate treatment" that would prevent "a new Jewish development"—a rising again of the Jewish people. In other words, those who were not killed by the tremendous difficulty of the work would need to be killed by other means.

When the Wannsee Conference closed, Himmler informed the chief inspector of the concentration camps to prepare to receive one hundred thousand Jewish men and fifty thousand Jewish women within the month.

Thus, the unsuccessful invasion of Russia brought radical changes to the concentration camp system. The prolonging of the fighting created a need for workers, but military failure slowed the flow of foreign prisoners to the labor pool. The frustration and hardships of a losing military campaign fueled a willingness to regard the Jews as scapegoats, as the cause of national suffering. After the Wannsee Conference in January 1942, the principal inmates of the concentration camps, instead of political enemies and prisoners of war, were Jews. The purpose of the camps, instead of detention, was forced labor. The method of operation, instead of intimidation, was exploitation. The ultimate fate of inmates, instead of eventual release, was usually death.

Types of Labor

To fit the camps for their economic mission, some companies were invited to place their operations either on or next to the camp grounds. Inside Auschwitz, for example, the I. G. Farben chemical giant produced fuel and synthetic rubber; Krupps Steel manufactured tanks, guns, and ammunition; and four hundred other industries assembled war materials. The Siemans Electric Corporation located plants in Auschwitz and in Ravensbrück, a women's camp, and "employed" workers from other camps as well. In an underground installation at Flossenbürg, inmates put aircraft together. The war industry set up factories near Buchenwald, Sachsenhausen, and Neuengamme. Some camps were near mines, from which internees extracted the metals they forged into weapons. Camp labor built warplanes for Messerschmitt and Heinkel and automobiles for Bavarian Motor Works (BMW) and Daimler-Benz. Concentration camp inmates manufactured dynamite to be used on their countrymen, assembled bombs that could destroy their homes, and sewed uniforms for their captors.

In addition to building the weapons of war, concentration camp inmates constructed or restored the facilities that enabled the soldiers to continue to fight. Laborers from camps in eastern Poland drained the marshes along the Russian front and built fortifications there. Other workers repaired bridges, airfields, roads,

Once the war started, prisoners were forced to work to supply necessities for the war. Concentration camps throughout Europe were established for forced labor. Inmates at the Mauthausen concentration camp were forced to labor to the point of exhaustion.

and railroad tracks that had been bombed. Prisoners from Theresienstadt constructed an underground military fortress.[5]

Inmates of camps close to the battlefront were assigned dangerous tasks. They carried ammunition to the front lines and set tank traps to slow the opposing army's advance. At least thirty thousand Russian prisoners were forced to operate antiaircraft guns aimed at Russian planes.[6]

Weapons production was the primary "employment" of concentration camp internees, but it was not the only form of exploitation. The expansion of the system required the enlargement of some camps and the addition of many others. Camp labor was used to build barracks that would house an ever increasing number of workers. Any upkeep of the camps' buildings or grounds was also performed by inmates.

The camps in Germany "hired out" their laborers to companies that needed to replace workers who were serving in the military. At Dachau, for example, internees who did not work in the weapons plant inside the camp were marched to nearby towns for various work details. Some toiled in a paper factory in the city of Dachau; some made porcelain for a company in the city of Allach. A great number were placed in armaments-production facilities. Many tended farms just outside the camp.

Deaths in the Labor Camps

These work camps, because of their unquestionably deplorable conditions, the unbearable rigors of their forced labor, and the unconscionable brutality of their guards, became death camps. Inmates perished in different ways.

The buildings were not heated, and blankets, coats, and even clothing were in short supply. One group of six hundred women in Buchenwald were dressed only in sacks with holes cut out for their arms and heads.[7] What shoes internees had when they arrived wore out quickly, and workers marched to and from their assignments in bare feet in both summer and winter. At Neubrandenburg, Aryan prisoners of war were given, by the commandant's order, the clothing and personal belongings of Jewish inmates, leaving the Jews barely more than undergarments for their bodies and nothing for their feet.[8] Thousands died from the bitter cold.

Food was also scarce. At Dachau, men received each day a thin slice of bread, a small piece of sausage or cheese, and cabbage or turnip soup.[9] At Lansdorf, one loaf of bread was to be divided among six or eight men; at Rathorn, a loaf of bread and half a jar of soup had to last five men two days.[10] Workers at Majdanek survived daily on a bowl of soup and less than eight ounces of bread.[11] Rations at Buchenwald consisted of a single piece of brown bread with a dab of margarine and a small serving of stew.[12] Thousands died from starvation.

The camps were miserably overcrowded and dirty beyond imagination. In some, five people slept in each wooden bunk. In Nogerratstrasse, prisoners were crammed into dog kennels nine feet long, six feet wide, and three feet high. In Kramerplatz, twelve hundred inmates shared ten toilets.[13] The supply of water to some camps was intermittent and to some nonexistent. Soap was seldom available and medicines were rare. The filthy conditions bred fleas, lice, rats, and sickness, and diseases raced through the crowded quarters of weakened inmates. Any illness quickly became an epidemic. Thousands died from typhus, dysentery, and other plagues.

If the forced labor was not in and of itself murderously backbreaking, it was made to be so. Internees worked twelve-hour shifts six days a week, usually at strenuous tasks without adequate equipment. At Mauthausen, barefoot prisoners carried stones weighing sixty pounds or more up the 168 rocky "steps of death" from the bottom of the quarry to the top, three hundred feet above—or to wherever they fell along the way.[14] Emaciated workers at Dachau were goaded with whips and bludgeons to load wagons with crushed rock so quickly they collapsed.[15] Those who toiled in the Farben works of Monowitz, a subsidiary camp of Auschwitz, rarely lived longer than three or four months. Thousands died from exhaustion.

The vicious savagery of the camp personnel is what kept the labor camps functioning as death camps. The commandants understood their charge to work their prisoners until they died of "natural" causes: exposure to the elements, undernourishment, disease, or physical weakness. And they carried out their orders. Inmates were kicked and beaten into working faster and harder. They were given impossible tasks to perform and flogged when they did not produce. If they showed the slightest defiance, their arms were pulled behind them, their hands tied, and they were hung by their wrists from trees or poles. Dachau inmates on the farmwork detail who were too ill or weak to work were marched into a lake and kept there until they succumbed to "natural causes."[16]

Labor camps that were set up throughout Europe were used mainly to help the Nazi war effort. Prisoners (top) at forced labor in the quarries at the Flossenbürg concentration camp. Prisoners (bottom) cutting stones.

43

Dachau Concentration Camp

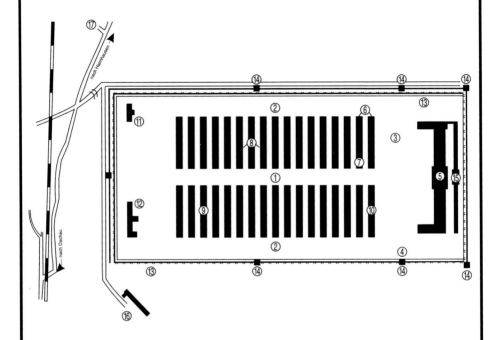

1. The main camp road, lined with poplar trees planted by prisoners
2. Blocks or barracks that housed prisoners
3. The *Appellplatz*—roll call area
4. The only entrance
5. Kitchen, laundry, storage rooms, torture rooms
6. Infirmary barracks
7. Morgue
8. Punishment barracks separated from others by barbed wire
9. Block 26 for clergymen
10. Canteen
11. Disinfection barracks
12. Camp garden
13. Ditch, electrified barbed wire fence, and wall
14. Watchtowers
15. Camp prison
16. Crematorium
17. Rifle range (for executions)

Often, those who could not be broken by any other means were simply executed. Camp officials had no difficulty finding offenses. A look or a word could be construed as "provoking rebellion" or "sabotage," crimes punishable by death. "Guilty" parties were shot or hanged.

Death was everywhere in the camps. If one inmate attempted to escape, twenty-five would be killed to keep others from trying the same thing. When the camp infirmaries—sick rooms, not hospitals—were full with people who were not likely to recover quickly, the sickest were executed to make room for those who might prove more productive. To escape the torture of living, men threw themselves against the electric fences or hanged themselves from their bunks.

The soaring death toll gave rise to a new concentration camp industry: the Death Brigade. At first, mass killings required no afterthought; bodies were simply buried in pits. But eventually, even the gaping graves could hold no more. Then the corpses were burned on large, open pyres. Finally, in 1940, crematoriums were installed. These were huge ovens in which human bodies could be reduced to ashes. By mid-1942, some inmates were assigned to the Death Brigades. Known as *Sonderkommandos*, they stripped the dead bodies of their fellow prisoners of anything of value—jewelry, hair, gold teeth—and carted their remains to the furnaces of the crematoriums for disposal.

Labor "Recruitment"

Because the death rate in the concentration camps was so high, new workers were continually needed. Germany impressed into its service a total of more than 7 million slave laborers. They were "recruited" from conquered towns. Squadrons of SS stationed themselves outside synagogues or other meeting places and, when people

45

The living conditions were literally unbearable in the camps. The prisoners were forced to work, often without food. Inmates often died from starvation and exhaustion.

emerged, loaded them into trucks marked "Worker Resettlement." Sometimes they barricaded the Jewish sector of cities and took every able-bodied person they found there. If they encountered resistance, they set fire to the homes and stores and seized all who tried to escape. One German Army unit—not an SS group— scoured Russia for "forty to fifty thousand youths from the age of ten to fourteen." Their plan was to "transport them to the Reich . . . for the alleviation of the shortage of apprentices" in German industries.[17]

A survivor of Budzyn, a satellite camp of Majdanek, described a typical instance of labor recruitment. Fifty inmates of the camp were taken to a small town to witness the capture of their fellow Jews. The Jewish quarter of the village was surrounded and machine guns fired randomly into houses. Everyone was ordered to assemble in the open square next to the synagogue, and any who fled were shot. The strongest people were crammed into transport trucks and the others locked up in the house of worship. Cans of gasoline were thrown, guns fired, and the retreating witnesses watched the synagogue explode in flames.[18]

Although the labor-camp system was very effective in ridding Germany of many of its Jews, the Nazis were capable of a far more sinister, far more efficient method. Years earlier, Hitler had quietly experimented with eliminating another group of people. That project had given him the rationale, the plan, and the technology for making the entire Reich *Judenrein* by the end of the war. The camps, with their hundreds of thousands of Jews, were perfect places to implement the fiendish scheme. The final solution to the Jewish question would require a new type of concentration camp.

4

The Extermination Camps

The Nazi doctrine of Aryan supremacy created a classification of people who were "unfit"—unfit for work, for social contact, for life itself. Some who fell into this category were the mentally ill, the physically handicapped, the incurably sick, and the aged. Hitler, in his callous, pragmatic way, devised a means of removing the unfit from his country's hospitals: euthanasia, or "mercy killing." In October 1939, perhaps to make room to treat wounded soldiers, Hitler signed a secret order permitting doctors "to grant a mercy death" to any patient who did not appear able to recover. He backdated the order to September 1, the date the slaughter of war began. The code name for this clandestine project was T4, after the address from which it was coordinated, Tiergartenstrasse 4 in Berlin—Hitler's office.

Six euthanasia centers were established in remote areas throughout Germany. In these buildings, isolated from the rest of the world, more than fifty thousand people judged "incurable" were "humanely" killed and their corpses cremated.[1] Falsified death certificates were sent to their relatives. Doctors experimented with different methods of murder: carbon monoxide gas and injection with morphine, cyanide, and other agents. Gas chambers, developed by an SS officer, were installed at each center.

Himmler recognized the usefulness of the T4 operation to the concentration camps. The large-scale killing that was possible at the euthanasia centers was more efficient and less messy than the mass executions by firing squad that were commonplace at the camps. Rather than waiting for inmates who were barely alive to succumb to "natural death," the SS could have the weakest declared unfit and shipped off to a euthanasia institute. They could even have political prisoners branded as mentally defective. Indeed, some psychiatric evaluation forms from Dachau and Ravensbrück listed as symptoms of mental disability "hostile to Germans," "insolent," "anti-German disposition," "Communist."[2] By mid-1941, T4 doctors were examining internees in different camps and sentencing them to death in the euthanasia centers. This process was euphemistically referred to by camp personnel as "special treatment," and the trucks that carried the victims to the killing centers were known as "invalid transports."

In the concentration camp records, the T4 operation became 14 f 13. In the precise and prolific paperwork of the Nazi regime, nearly everything was identified and documented. Death from natural causes was 14 f 1, suicide was 14 f 2. A notation of 14 f 3 meant the prisoner was shot during an escape attempt. Execution was 14 f L.[3] "Special treatment" was accorded to individuals of every population in the camp: Russians, Poles, Gypsies, asocials. Jews, however, were selected

for the invalid transports as a group, and they comprised the bulk of the victims. Exactly how many people perished in the 14 f 13 project in the concentration camps will never be known because many of the carefully kept records were destroyed, but the figure is probably at least twenty thousand.[4]

Once the directors of the concentration-camp system embarked on a path of deliberate and barely disguised racial murder, each next step was logical, however twisted the logic had become. After legitimizing the killing of "unfit" people in euthanasia institutes and rationalizing the transfer of undesirables to those institutes, the obvious next move was to bring the medical murder directly to the camp. Then it was but a small step to establish facilities for which the sole purpose would be slaughter, not of isolated individuals, but of an entire race of people deemed unfit to live: the Jews. Four extermination camps were built in 1941 and 1942, and two existing camps were reconstructed to become both labor camp and killing center.

The code name for the policy of eliminating the Jewish problem by wholesale murder of all Jews was Operation Reinhard, after Reinhard Heydrich, the German security officer responsible for implementing the final solution. The way it worked was that Jews in the ghettos of Poland and some of the captured Russian territories would be "resettled in the East" and Jews

Elizabeth Killiam (top), age twenty-three and the mother of twins, was sterilized by Nazis before being transferred to a euthanasia center. Hundreds of thousands of mentally impaired people were put to death through Hitler's euthanasia program, such as the patients (bottom) in the Schoenbrunn asylum near Dachau.

from Germany transported to the vacated ghettos. After a few days or weeks, the ghettos were again emptied "to the East" and more German Jews relocated to the ghettos. The process was to be repeated until no Jew remained in the Reich. Beneath all the deceitful language about "crossing the frontier" and "resettlement transports" was the unspoken reality that "the East" meant the death camps.

The extermination camps were all located in the eastern part of Poland, where they were far from any criticism from German citizens. A public outcry against the euthanasia institutes had forced Hitler to put an end to the gassings in Germany. Germans had not objected to the persecution and deportation of Jews, but there was no need to test their response to large-scale racial extermination.

By late 1941, the vast majority of Europe's Jews were located in Poland and Russia, lands Hitler had targeted for German *Lebensraum*. Eastern Poland, near the Russian border, was an ideal site for implementing the final solution. The large tracts of forested land located there could hide or camouflage death factories lest anyone object and try to shut them down. A good railroad system provided easy access to almost any area. Many Poles were intensely anti-Semitic and would probably close their eyes to the torture of Jews. Although many other groups of people were interned throughout the Reich-held territory and became victims of Nazi fury, the Jews had been singled out not simply for harsh treatment but for annihilation.

Chelmno

The first extermination camp was located in a large, mansionlike house outside the small, isolated village of Chelmno. Nicknamed the Palace, it was far enough from cities or towns so as to keep its business fairly

Starting in 1933, the Nazis began to set up concentration camps throughout Europe. Originally established for political prisoners of the Reich, they eventually were turned into camps for millions of Jews. By the early 1940s, the entire purpose of some of the camps was extermination.

secret, yet a road and a feeder railway line permitted trucks and trains to bring victims right to the gate. The inhabitants of Chelmno were removed from the area—all but a few men, who were used to build two wooden barracks and a high fence. Only two barracks were erected because the facility was not meant to house people for any length of time. Extermination was to take place as soon after arrival as possible, for that was the entire purpose of the camp.

Chelmno had no permanent gas chamber. Instead, it used five vans that could hold 100 to 150 people each. The vehicles were equipped so that their carbon-monoxide exhaust emptied into the section carrying passengers, asphyxiating them. Its first operation took place December 8, 1941. As the transports arrived, the victims—primarily but not entirely Jews from the surrounding villages—were greeted by SS officers dressed in white coats, with stethoscopes draped around their necks. The "doctors" carefully recorded the items each person had brought, promising to hold them while the prisoners showered and were deloused. Following the To the Bath sign, these first arrivals climbed a ramp into a van, some of which were made to look like the mercy trucks of the Red Cross.[5] The mobile gas chamber then headed into the thick woods. If the driver accelerated gradually, death came slowly, peacefully. More commonly, the executioner stepped heavily on the pedal, bringing a quick and terrifying end from asphyxiation.[6]

At first, Chelmno had no crematorium. When screams no longer came from the van, the driver drove to one of several open pits in the forest that were already filling with rotting corpses. Jewish prisoners of the *Sonderkommando*—the Death Brigade—pulled the lifeless bodies from the van and stacked them neatly in the communal grave. Eventually, the poisonous fumes and the stench from these burial pits forced installation of a crematorium. At that time, the SS commissioned the *Sonderkommando* to exhume all the corpses buried in the forest and burn them in the furnace.

Most of the victims killed at Chelmno were from the nearby Lodz ghetto. The Palace was in operation only fifteen months, from December 1941 to March 1943, and reopened briefly as the war drew to a close. In that time, at least five thousand Gypsies, about one hundred thousand Jews, and thousands of others[7]—perhaps three hundred forty thousand in all[8]—perished there.

Belzec

On March 17, 1942, three months after Chelmno began operation, the second extermination camp opened. Belzec was located just off the main railroad line between two provinces containing many ghettos: Lublin and Lvov. It was the first camp with stationary gas chambers. At first, the operation was small: three gas chambers in three wooden barracks made to look like bathhouses. Each could hold about 750 people.[9] In June, the capacity for killing was enlarged: the wooden barracks were replaced by brick buildings and the number of gas chambers increased to six. Evacuees from the ghettos were herded into the chambers and carbon-monoxide gas was pumped in. When canisters of gas proved inefficient, fuel exhaust from a diesel engine was used.

The facilities at Belzec were crude and broke down frequently. Many times victims waited for days, crammed in railroad cars without food or water. When the wait was over, they were locked in the crowded gas chambers, sometimes for as long as three hours, while their captors struggled to start the engine.

Belzec continued to function despite its difficulties until about November 1942. In those eight months, probably five hundred thousand people were killed. It took the Jewish *Sonderkommando* another seven months to pull the corpses from their shared graves, stack them on iron or wooden frames, and burn away every trace of their lives and their deaths.

55

Jews were not the only target of the Nazis. Gypsy prisoners, awaiting instructions from their German captors, sit in an open area near the fence in the Belzec concentration camp.

Sobibór

A third camp, Sobibór, was modeled after Belzec. Like its prototype, this camp, concealed by thick woods along the Bug River, began small in May 1942 and added new equipment four months later. Jews came from as far as Holland for "special treatment" there—34,313 of them from that one country alone. Only nineteen survived and returned to their homes.[10]

As soon as the packed trains opened their doors, twenty to eighty of the men who were still alive were separated from the rest. They were permitted to live for a week or more to tend to the tasks of sorting the personal belongings the prisoners would have stripped from them, moving dead bodies to make room for the condemned, and disposing of the remains of their friends and loved ones. A few girls from each transport were marched to the tailoring workshops of the outer camps, where they transformed the clothing of their neighbors into coats and uniforms for their oppressors. Every other man, woman, and child went directly to the gas chambers. An estimated two hundred fifty thousand perished at Sobibór.

Treblinka

The last camp whose sole purpose was extermination was only fifty miles from the large city of Warsaw. A labor camp was already in operation at Treblinka, bringing gravel from nearby quarries. It became known as Treblinka I when the death camp, Treblinka II, was built. Treblinka II opened July 23, 1942, primarily for the "resettlement" of the Jews in the Warsaw ghetto. But the three small gas chambers, which operated on the exhaust of captured Russian tanks and trucks, were not ready when the first trainloads arrived. So the guards simply machine-gunned their victims as they spilled onto the railroad platform.

By March, ten new gas chambers had been installed that could each hold two hundred people at a time, and the camp was running fairly efficiently.[11] In order to conceal the camp's purpose from its victims for as long as possible, the unloading platform had been made to look like any other railway station, with schedules and timetables and advertisements posted. The road that ran the few yards from the "station" to the gas chambers went past empty buildings that appeared to be thriving stores and shops. But no adornment could disguise the camp's mission for long. Every day, five thousand Jews were transported from Warsaw to

Treblinka. Thousands came from other ghettos also. Between the inhumane conditions in the cattle cars, the executions, and the gas chambers, over eight hundred thousand died at Treblinka.[12]

Chelmno, Belzec, Sobibór, and Treblinka were created purely for the annihilation of the Jews. The two other extermination centers began as prison and labor camps. They had been established in what was then the farthest reaches of German conquest to serve as outposts for continued expansion.

Majdanek

Majdanek, unlike the four other death camps, was not hidden from the eyes of the world. It occupied over one hundred acres on a flat, treeless expanse of land on the edge of the city of Lublin, Poland. When the "resettled" Jews of the ghettos were shipped to their deaths, the "usable" ones were sent to Majdanek, where their labor could contribute to the German economy for a short time. At the end of 1942, gas chambers were in use in Majdanek, but executions took place on a much larger scale when new chambers were installed in April 1943. Even the added facilities were not sufficient to satisfy the murderous cravings of the captors, for large groups were commonly marched to wooded areas and shot en masse.

Although Majdanek was operated as an extermination camp, probably 60 percent of the deaths there were from brutal work conditions, starvation, and disease. Less than half of the killings were by gas. In its three years, Majdanek claimed the lives of nearly two hundred thousand people.

Auschwitz

By far the largest of the annihilation camps was Auschwitz. In 1939, before the German Army overran

Poland, Auschwitz was a lonely, fog-shrouded industrial town on the banks of the Vistula and Sola rivers. It was on a main railway line but far from any village or city—easily accessible but relatively isolated, the perfect place for especially violent Polish prisoners. A group of internees from Dachau was brought to transform an old cavalry barracks into a high-security prison. Thus, Auschwitz began not as a death camp for Jews, but as a prison camp for Poles.

The commandant, Rudolf Höss, was well suited for the role of master warden, having served five years in prison for murder before being released by the Nazi government. As an SS corporal, he had worked in two other concentration camps, first Dachau and then Sachsenhausen. He brought thirty German prisoners who had been held as criminals at Sachsenhausen to function as guards and opened the camp on June 14, 1940, to receive 728 Poles who had been arrested by the Gestapo.

In addition to a prison, Auschwitz was envisioned as an outstation for German colonization of Poland and, eventually, Russia. The inmates were put to work clearing and taming the marshy land in preparation for Aryan settlers. They established and manned an agricultural station, where they experimented with different crops and farming techniques. And, because the anticipated colonies would need industry, German companies set up shop in and around the camp. Thus, two years before the transformation of the concentration camp system from detention centers to labor pools, Auschwitz had become a work camp.

As Hitler's army was preparing to invade Russia, Himmler was readying his concentration camps to receive the large numbers of prisoners of war that were expected. He ordered Auschwitz dramatically expanded (Auschwitz I) and a second camp built in the village of Birkenau two miles away—large enough to accommodate one hundred thousand men and women (Auschwitz II). I. G. Farben, the chemical manufacturing company that "employed" twenty-seven thousand to thirty thousand inmates, constructed a third facility at Monowitz, which coordinated about forty smaller camps that dotted the surrounding countryside for miles (Auschwitz III). The massive complex, which housed as many as one hundred thirty thousand people at a time in severely crowded barracks, was the largest in the entire system.

Months before the "final solution" became the official, although unwritten, policy, Auschwitz had been selected as the primary site for its implementation. Its remote location hid its activities from any prying eyes. Its location on a main rail line from Katowice to Krakow made the transport of thousands of people a day feasible. The four hundred industries in and around its buildings camouflaged the smokestacks of its furnaces and fooled many victims into believing the Worker Resettlement signs on the cattle cars that arrived regularly.

The deliberate killing began in the summer of 1941, before any of the other extermination camps were even built. At first, the murders were performed outside the camp. Russian and Polish war prisoners classified as

Gas chambers were installed in concentration camps in order to murder Jews more efficiently and in larger numbers. The crematoriums were built to destroy the dead bodies. Selection of Hungarian Jews (top) at the Auschwitz-Birkenau ramp. Construction of Crematorium II (bottom) at Birkenau.

sick or otherwise unable to work were transported to the Sonnerstein euthanasia center. There they were either gassed or had phenol, a powerful, fast-acting poison derived from coal tar, injected into their bloodstreams or their hearts.

By September, the operation was brought to the camp—to the building known as Block 11. On September 3, six hundred invalid Russian POWs and 250 of the sickest from the camp infirmary were packed into the basement of the prison block and crystals of Zyklon B, the pesticide and disinfectant hydrogen cyanide, were thrown through the door before it was locked shut. A few days later, nine hundred more were massacred in the same way.

Extermination on a large scale, however, did not begin until almost a year later (July 1942), when Operation Reinhard was in full swing. Two farmhouses at Birkenau were gutted, insulated, and equipped with gas vents. Their first victims were people already condemned by a typhus epidemic that had raged throughout the entire camp.

But these makeshift chambers were inadequate to handle the size of transports of intended Jewish victims. Over the course of the next year, four gassing/crematorium complexes were manufactured specifically for Auschwitz II (Birkenau) and installed at the western edge of the camp compound.

Crematoriums II and III (Crematorium I was the existing facility in the main camp) each had underground gas chambers connected by lifts to fifteen ovens in aboveground rooms that could dispose of 1,440 bodies a day. In Crematoriums IV and V, the gas chambers were on the same floor as the furnaces; in each, 768 corpses could be carted by rail wagon to eight ovens each day. The daily capacity of the five installations was 4,756. Auschwitz commandant Höss once boasted that he was personally responsible for the murders of 2.5 million people at the camp.[13]

The actual number of people who were given "special treatment" at Auschwitz will never be known. Even the Nazi bureaucracy that compulsively maintained detailed records of all their deeds could not keep up with the human flood that spilled through the gates of its largest camp. From many transports, the names and numbers of untold thousands who went directly to their doom were not even entered on the rolls.

Other Camps

In Operation Reinhard, the six killing centers received and disposed of Jews from nearly every country in continental Europe. In addition to transports from Poland and Russia and Germany, trains came from Hungary, Romania, Czechoslovakia, Bulgaria, and Yugoslavia. Jews were brought from Austria, Italy, France, and Greece. Holland, Belgium, Finland, Norway, and Luxembourg also lost portions of their Jewish populations to the death factories in Poland.

In order to bring hundreds of thousands of Jews from these countries to their deaths in Poland, transit camps were set up throughout Nazi-occupied Europe. The transit camps were holding areas where Jews waited for the cattle cars that would carry them to Auschwitz or Sobibór. From Drancy, outside Paris, France, sixty-one thousand Jews went to Auschwitz. From Westerbork, in northern Holland, more than eighty-eight thousand Jews were transported to the extermination camps.

Throughout Russia, many of the labor camps became annihilation centers, saving the Nazis the trouble of transporting Jews. In Transnistria, a province in

the Ukraine governed by Romania, concentration camps disposed of tens of thousands of Romanian Jews.

Procedure

For all the victims, the procedure was ghastly. First came the transport to the camp. Jews were rounded up in their native lands and held in the transit camps until room could be made for them in the annihilation centers in Poland. Then they were packed into boxcars with no regard for anything except the number of bodies that could be crammed into the available space. They made the journey without food or water, sometimes with a single bucket to suffice for all sanitation needs. Openings in the freight cars were covered with barbed wire, and anyone who managed to claw through the wire and jump from the train was shot and left by the side of the track. Hundreds suffocated or starved before reaching their destination. In some trains, as many as 80 percent died in transit.[14]

At the camp, the cars emptied onto the disembarking ramp, where guards with whips and dogs organized the new arrivals. As the line paraded past a "doctor," each person was ordered either to the right or the left. Those on the right marched toward the ovens. Some were automatically shunted to the right: anyone older than forty or fifty, anyone who looked

At Auschwitz (top), an orchestra made up of inmates performs at the departure and return of work battalions. This photograph was used as evidence in the trial of Rudolf Höss. Human remains (bottom) found by American troops in the crematoria ovens in Buchenwald.

frail or weak, and all the children. Those few on the left were consigned to a slower death. At Auschwitz and Majdanek, they were sentenced to work details, and at any of the six camps they might be assigned to the Death Brigade.

In the sanitized vocabulary that pervaded the Third Reich, the process of choosing who would die now and who would die later was called "selection." The executions were referred to as "special treatment," "delousing," "disinfecting," or "special action." Dropping the Zyklon B crystals into the vents that protruded from the neatly kept lawn was "giving them something to chew on." The euphemisms were necessary for two reasons. First, they concealed for a time the grisly truth from the victims and thus made enforcement easier. People entered Resettlement Transports and Shower Rooms with much less coercion when they did not realize what awaited them there. Second, the less offensive words permitted the executioners to somehow delude themselves into lessening the severity of their unspeakable deeds in their own minds. The evasive terminology "detoxified killing and aided in its routinization."[15]

In accordance with the practice of masking reality until the last possible moment, inmate orchestras sometimes serenaded the condemned to the gas chambers with happy, lilting melodies. Before entering the shower rooms, victims undressed completely. Females had their hair shorn. They were told that this was the first step in a delousing procedure, for they would not want lice to spoil their new quarters. In reality, the hair was to be made into mattresses for the comfort of German soldiers, socks for U-boat crews, and felt footwear for the Reich's railway workers.[16] Sometimes the victims were given soap or towels to bolster the charade.

Once the gas chambers were full, either carbon monoxide was pumped in (at Chelmno, Belzec, Sobibór, and Treblinka) or Zyklon B crystals were fed into the vents (at Majdanek and Auschwitz). Within ten to thirty minutes, the chamber was silent and still. About a half hour later, fans pumped out the poisoned air and the *Sonderkommandos* of the Death Brigade donned gas masks and rubber boots for their grisly work.

First, they hosed the bodies clean of the blood and feces that accompanied such ghastly death. Then with ropes, hooks, and rags, they separated the stiffening bodies. Theirs was the task of removing rings from the fingers of corpses and pulling gold fillings from their mouths. When nothing of value was left, they moved the remains to the furnaces. The pieces of bone and teeth the fire could not destroy were then ground in a mill until all that remained of each human life was a bit of fine ash, which was scattered into nearby rivers and streams.

Other workers sifted through the clothing and other belongings piled near the doors of the gas chambers. Each piece was examined thoroughly for hidden valuables. Wooden barrels were used for sorting jewelry, timepieces, pocketknives, eyeglasses, umbrellas, combs, flashlights, and hundreds of other articles. With typical Nazi efficiency, every item was recorded, its value assigned, and its use and destination determined. Money and gold were sent to the Reich Central Bank, watches and ink pens were set aside for gifts for SS men and Nazi soldiers, and clothing was shipped to Germany.

When the number of victims that survived the transport was too few to fill a gas chamber, they were dispatched instead by a bullet in the back of the head. When the number was larger than the crematoriums could handle, the living and the dead were burned together in open trenches.

The six extermination camps were distinguished from the other concentration camps only by virtue of the fact that their primary objective was racial annihilation. But death was a prominent feature in all the camps—the prison camps, the labor camps, and even the transit camps. Death simply came by various means. It came every day in every camp in every imaginable form. Every camp was a death camp.

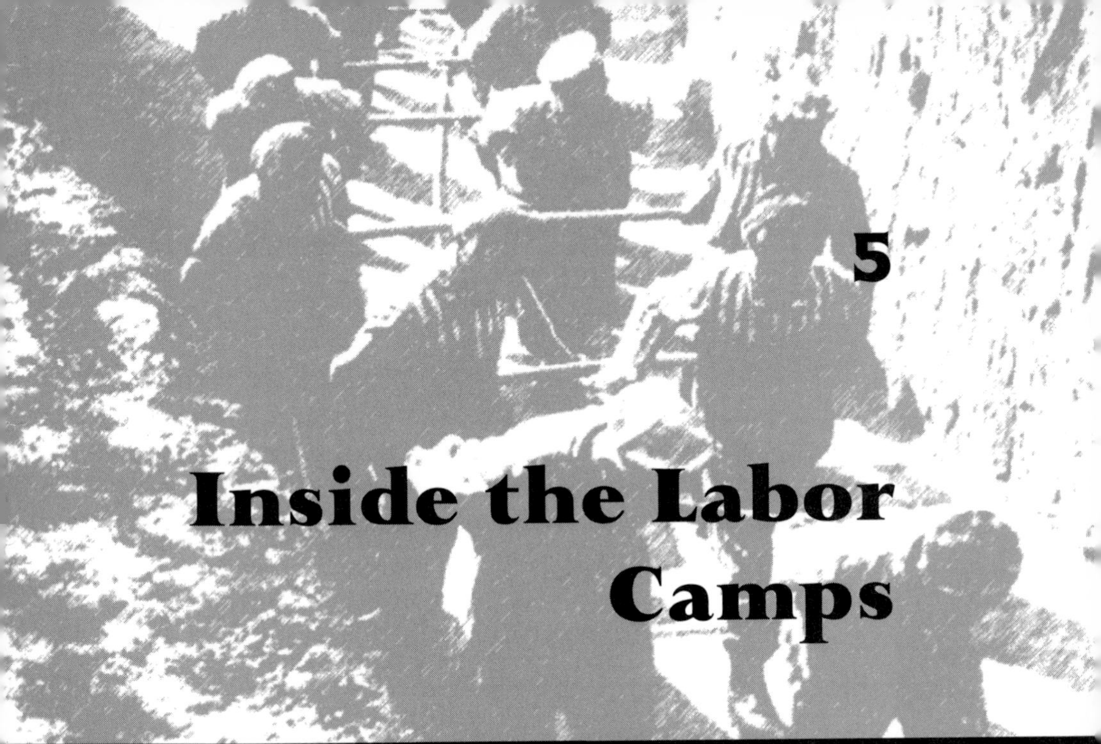

5

Inside the Labor Camps

"The SS rarely murdered anyone."[1] This bitter comment was made by a Dachau survivor about life inside the prison/labor camp. He was right. In the labor camps, the SS themselves did little of the actual killing. The rulers of the concentration camp empire exercised their authority through an ingenious system of indirect control. They made the rules and determined the penalties for breaking them, but they used the most ruthless of the prisoners to enforce the rules and mete out punishment.

The camp commandant was, of course, an SS officer. But he appointed the most hardened criminal interned there as the camp senior, who was responsible for the day-to-day operation of the camp. Under the camp senior was a carefully organized ladder of foremen, block leaders, cell leaders, secretaries, and other administrative functionaries—all prisoners. These were the people who had direct and immediate control over the lives of their fellow internees. In the camps in Germany, the internal organization was usually staffed by German criminal inmates; in Poland and Russia, these positions were often held by Ukrainian (southwest Russian) prisoners of war. Jews were never given such authority. The principal qualifications seem to have been a capacity—or, better, a lust—for brutality and a total disregard for the value of human life. Many professors, lawyers, doctors, priests, ministers, and rabbis were under the unrelenting thumb of thieves, rapists, and murderers.

Every camp had a chief of police and guards who belonged to the SS, but most of their work was done through the camp police. The camp was divided into blocks and cells, and each one was headed by a prisoner who had already demonstrated a willingness and an ability to treat others savagely. The work details were placed under equally corrupt inmate foremen known as *kapos*, probably from *capo*, the Italian word for "chief." (Some Italians were among the early prisoners in Dachau and may have introduced the word.)

The SS officer in charge of prison labor and of transports out of the camp—to the ghettos or extermination camps of Poland—worked through the Labor Allocation Office. This essential department was under the complete direction of prison staff. The SS officer decided how many people were needed for each work detail, and the Labor Allocation Office made the assignments. The SS command relayed the orders, stating how many were to be loaded on the next "invalid transport" or "resettlement" train, and the prisoners running the Labor Allocation Office chose the deportees.

The inmates who rose—or sank—to the coveted positions in this office had the power of life and death over their fellow prisoners. They decided not only who would be transported, eventually to the gas chambers, but also where individuals would work, which often determined their chances for survival. Some—usually other criminal prisoners—toiled in the upkeep of the camp, a fairly light task. Others marched to mines, stone quarries, armaments factories, and other places of hard labor, where life expectancy was seldom more than three months. Still others worked in agricultural details, where they could sometimes sneak a few bites of fresh produce and smuggle food back to the camp. A fourth group—limited to Jews—formed the *Sonderkommando*, whose members were generally killed and replaced regularly. In many camps, every detail of camp labor, from where individuals were placed to how they were treated, was subject to the caprice of those whose previous profession had been breaking the law.

Since they gave great authority to inmates, the SS officers made certain that the prison chiefs could not sabotage the camp operation. They mixed people of all nationalities together as much as possible and seeded the criminal prisoners among the political detainees. They encouraged inmates to inform on one another and rewarded spies with cigarettes, extra food, or special privileges.

Höss, the commandant of Auschwitz, called the concentration camp system of indirect control the "green-triangle aristocracy."[2] Inverted triangular patches of different colors were sewn on the uniforms of inmates to identify the reason for their internment. A red patch marked a political prisoner, including a prisoner of war. Black was for asocials, purple for Jehovah's Witnesses and other conscientious objectors, maroon for Gypsies, and pink for homosexuals. Habitual criminals wore green. For Jews, a triangle of whatever color indicated their "crime" was sewn on top of a point-up yellow triangle, forming the six-pointed Star of David that was universally associated with Judaism.

71

The colored patch was one form of inmate identification. Another was the number assigned each prisoner. It was printed on a patch and sewn above the triangle on the blue-and-white-striped, pajama-like uniform. In some camps, it was inked on the chest, and in others it was tattooed on the left forearm. Concentration camp internees did not have names; they had only numbers.

Camp Routine

Every day in the camps began with a wake-up call—at 5:00 A.M. in the winter and 4:00 A.M. in the summer. Sometimes prisoners could swallow a little coffee before assembling in the *Appellplatz*, the roll-call square. Here they arranged themselves in some camps by fives and in others by tens or in some other order, according to their numbers. In rain or shine, snow or hail, with shoes or without, they stood for an hour or more while their leaders accounted for each one. If one or two people were late to the lineup, the entire camp might be wakened an hour earlier the next day and made to stand an hour longer. Many of the prisoners were too weak to endure the long roll calls; some died from sheer exhaustion. Every morning after roll call, several bodies lay motionless on the *Appellplatz*.

At Dachau, the camp prototype where the schedule was originally established, the *Appellplatz* was between the barracks and the kitchen/laundry/storage facility.

The Nazis often took pictures, called "mug shots," of the concentration camp inmates. Each prisoner was given a number, which was often tattooed on his or her arm. The three young Jews pictured left were all prisoners at Auschwitz. Their fate is unknown.

As the prisoners stood at attention each morning, words painted in giant letters on the roof of the large building mocked them: "There is one road to freedom. Its milestones are: obedience, diligence, honesty, order, cleanliness, temperance, truth, sacrifice, and love of one's country."[3] Very few of the people who read that sign were allowed to take that road to freedom.

Morning rations—generally a small piece of bread for each internee—were distributed after roll call and people were divided among the various labor details. They worked twelve hours each day, from 6:00 or 7:00 in the morning until 6:00 or 7:00 at night, with a brief pause at noon for a meager meal. Every evening, the lifeless bodies of those who could not complete the day's assignment were dragged back to the camp.

As the work crews returned to camp, many passed another ironic sign. At Dachau and Auschwitz and several other camps, at the only entrance and exit over the ditch, through the wall, beneath the electrified wire, and past the guard towers, this lie was forged in the twisted metal of the gate: "Work Makes One Free." At Buchenwald, the sign on the gate was equally false and more foreboding: "Each Gets What He Deserves."

Evening roll call ended the day's labor. The exhausted, emaciated prisoners would stand rigid, hands at their sides, for another hour while every body was accounted for. If the evening count did not match the morning's—after adjustments for the day's known casualties—the wait would be longer. If anyone was missing and presumed escaped, a punishment roll call would last all night and half the next day. When the grueling ordeal was finally over, each inmate would be given a bit of bread, sometimes a slice of sausage or cheese, sometimes a cup of thin soup.[4] Then the prisoners would stumble numbly to their barracks.

The sign above the entrance gate to the Auschwitz death camp reads Arbeit Macht Frei *(Work Makes One Free). The prisoners were forced to work, but they were not freed.*

In some camps, this was a seven-day-a-week schedule. In others, Sundays provided a brief respite. At Budzyn, a subsidiary of Majdanek, prisoners performed plays on their one day off. At Flossenbürg, an orchestra composed entirely of inmates softened the harshness by playing tunes from Wagner and Beethoven on the *Appellplatz* on Sunday afternoons.[5] The same musicians, in several camps, were forced to play rousing melodies as crews marched to and from their day's torturous labor.

Those were not the only times the music sounded. At Auschwitz, the orchestra welcomed incoming transports. The Nazi overlords required the musicians to escort the condemned to the place of execution. And someone was shot or hanged every day. A word or an act that could be construed as insubordination was punishable by death. If a prisoner returned from a factory with any item—even a thimble—he was accused of sabotaging the war effort and was immediately killed. If an inmate escaped while on work detail, twenty-five others from his labor group would be shot in reprisal.

Physical Appearance

The most obvious physical features of the camps were the monotonous rows of wooden barracks. Each barrack, or block, typically contained four dormitory-like cells and two latrines. They were built for utility, not comfort. The only items of furniture in the unheated blocks were a table and benches (in some) and tiered platforms that served as bunks (in most). In some, there were no bunks—prisoners drew beds on the floor with chalk.[6] Most bunks had no mattresses—only straw.

New arrivals were ushered first to the disinfection barrack. Here they had their hair shaved off—the hair on their heads and all their body hair. They were kept in quarantine until they were pronounced healthy enough to enter the main camp and room was made for them in the miserably crowded blocks.

Prisoners of the camps were forced to endure daily roll calls. The prisoners had to stand, even in extreme weather, for hours at a time in complete silence. SS and police officials (top) speaking among themselves during a roll call of the prisoners. Newly arrived prisoners (bottom), their heads shaved and still in their civilian clothes, at roll call in Buchenwald concentration camp.

One or more barracks served as the camp infirmary. Prisoners who were sick enough to be allowed to go to the infirmary were often too ill to have much chance of recovery. The infirmary was not a hospital; it was a room where the very sick could be separated from the other internees. Prisoner doctors working with very crude instruments and too few supplies did what they could, but for most the infirmary was only a place where they could rest briefly. The rule was that no more than 10 percent of the camp population (5 percent at Monowitz) could be in the sick room. When the number of sick approached that figure, those closest to death were killed, usually by phenol injection, to make room for those who might live another day. Nazi efficiency had no room for unproductive people.

Another barrack was called the Bunker. Here resisters and recaptured escapees were interrogated and tortured. The yard outside the Bunker was the site for floggings and executions. At least one barrack served as a morgue, which was always full of bodies awaiting the incinerators. Every morning, the corpses of those who had collapsed at the evening roll call or who had not awakened from their sleep were brought here.

The crematorium was another ugly, omnipresent feature of camp life. Every camp had at least one. Even when the building that housed the furnaces was surrounded with trees and flowers, the smokestack could not be disguised. In the daylight, black smoke billowed from the chimneys; in the night, fire from the smokestacks lit up a blood-red sky.

Brutality

The greatest certainty in the concentration camp was death, and the second was the capricious savagery of the camp personnel. Block leaders beat those under their command with rubber hoses just to establish who was in charge. *Kapos* forced their labor crews to march briskly to their work site, then whipped and kicked any who could not keep pace. If one inmate was caught stealing a few potato peelings, his whole block's paltry rations might be cut in half. At Gusen, a group of men considered no longer useful were taken to a corner of the camp compound on a subzero February night, made to strip naked, and forced to stand at attention while their wardens pummelled them with bursts of icy water. They were left there to die of "natural causes." In the morning, the body-gathering crew picked up their corpses.[7]

At Dachau, the SS regularly conducted "rabbit hunts" to frighten political prisoners into revealing secrets the Nazis wanted. The guards called the numbers of ten or fifteen men, some political detainees they had no intention of killing and others expendable prisoners. The "rabbits" were lined up single file in the long, slim space between barracks. Each had a target pinned to his back, on the left side, directly behind his heart. All were ordered to "exercise"—to run the length of the narrow passageway. As they began, the SS men raised their guns. They shot only the unimportant runners, which was often enough to intimidate the political inmates into cooperation.[8]

More often than not, the cruelty served no purpose other than to satisfy the sadistic power-lust of depraved men. At Auschwitz, the green triangles once lined up ninety Jewish women in a third-floor room. As horrified inmates looked on, the men hurled them all through the window into the courtyard below.[9]

At Flossenbürg, new arrivals sat motionless, backs straight and hands flat on the table, when their first meal of watery soup was placed in front of them. If they spoke or moved, the rod of the block leader cracked across their backs or heads. Permission to eat was immediately followed by a command to leap under the table. Startled prisoners dropped their bowls and hurried to obey, spilling the only food they had been given. Within moments, they were ordered to return to their seats, hands again on the table. The entire exercise was repeated—and repeated and repeated and repeated for an hour, until precious little soup remained.[10]

The commander of the camp at Budzyn would watch the performances of the inmate drama groups, applaud as though he had seen nothing better, then empty his submachine gun on the actors. On Sunday, the one day no one went to the rock quarry, the commander would roar through the camp on his motorcycle as internees were eating lunch outside and pepper the crowd with bullets from his weapon. Dozens of men would fall, dead or wounded, and soup would squirt from holes in the serving barrels. Whipping was seldom sufficient punishment to satisfy him; he often took prisoners who had offended him in any way, however slight, roped them behind his horse, and galloped triumphantly around the camp.[11]

Selections

The "selection" became a daily, sometimes twice daily, reality of life in the camps after the introduction of Operation Reinhard. At this time, severe overcrowding strained resources well beyond the camps' limits, so it was decided that prisoner ranks had to be thinned. Once official policy not only sanctioned but actually demanded Judeocide, murder was carried out in typically systematic fashion. In the barracks or at roll call, an inspector walked in and out among the rows of naked, skeletal inmates and "selected" the required number for "transfer"—to an extermination camp, to an infirmary where lethal injection syringes awaited

Prisoners standing on the Appellplatz *during a roll call. Each wears a striped hat and uniform bearing colored, triangular badges and identification numbers.*

them, or to a firing squad and mass burial pit. Doctors were used to make the selections in order to give the illusion of legitimacy to the procedure. They had no choice but to assign some criteria to their decisions. They looked for people who seemed especially weak, or who wrapped bandages over wounds, or who had boils or sores or rashes or merely scars. One examiner used the thickness of men's thighs as his gauge: If a prisoner's legs were so thin that the doctor's fist could fit between them without touching skin, the inmate did not have muscle enough to remain in the labor force.[12]

The inmates understood the significance of the in-camp selections, and those who retained the human instinct to survive devised methods of holding on to their lives a little longer. One woman washed her face, brushed her teeth, and forced her mouth into a smile so that she would appear strong. Others rubbed their cheeks vigorously to produce the rosy illusion of health. When selections were made with prisoners clothed, they crammed rags under their uniforms to fill out their frail frames.[13]

Some internees were so emaciated they were barely alive. They were known as Mussulmen. The word meant "Muslim," and the name came from the appearance of a group of prisoners, sitting in a bent-over, prayerlike posture, each with a scrap of blanket draped around thin shoulders, awaiting death. Because Mussulmen seldom had the strength to live for more than a few days, poison gas was usually not wasted on them.

Medical Experiments

Some in-camp selections did not end immediately with execution; some prisoners were selected for medical experimentation. The twisted logic of the Nazi medical world suggested that concentration camp inmates, who were already marked for death, would be superior to animal subjects in scientific research. In fact, one doctor admitted, "For me there was no basic difference . . . between Jews and guinea pigs."[14] Some experiments were conducted to gain information that might help soldiers on the battlefront, such as how the human body reacts to changes in altitude, air pressure, and temperature. Others simply satisfied morbid curiosity or were done in hopes that a discovery or a research study would advance some doctor's professional career.

The experimentation began with a May 15, 1941, letter to Heinrich Himmler from Dr. Sigmund Rascher. The doctor had just learned that research on the effects of high altitude on airplane pilots could not proceed because "no tests with human material had yet been possible as such experiments are very dangerous and nobody volunteers for them."[15] He knew expendable subjects were available in the concentration camps, and he asked permission to use them, observing that "the subjects can, of course, die." Himmler responded, "Prisoners will, of course, be made available gladly."[16]

Rascher set up his laboratory at Dachau and for three years subjected internees there to unbelievably harrowing ordeals. In addition to the high-altitude tests, exposure experiments were conducted in tanks of water cooled to 2.5°C (36.5°F) and in ice and snow (with subjects naked) at -6°C (21.2°F).[17] Rascher also tested different medicines for the treatment of various diseases. He infected inmates with malaria and other diseases and then administered the experimental antidote. In almost every case, he found that his "biochemical treatment has hardly any effect."[18] Yet he continued. Rascher documented hundreds of experiments at Dachau.

At Buchenwald, Gypsies were fed nothing but saltwater to see how long a person might survive with only ocean water to drink. Women at Ravensbrück were used to test methods of bone grafting.[19] At Mauthausen, doctors experimented with different drugs for tuberculosis.[20] A doctor and professor at Natzweiler kept a collection of Jewish skulls for anthropology research. At Neuengamme, twenty Jewish children, some as young as five, were infected with tuberculosis in fruitless research.[21]

The most infamous of the SS doctors was Josef Mengele, chief medical officer of Auschwitz, dubbed the Angel of Death by inmates. He made most of the selections on the ramp, standing regally erect and moving only his riding crop or one white-gloved finger to the right or left as the new arrivals paraded endlessly

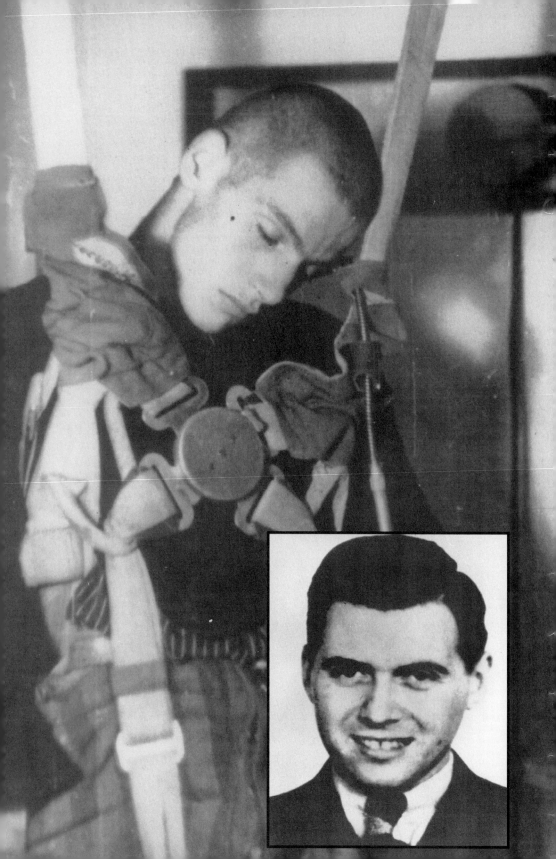

past. He performed or oversaw most of the lethal injections. He personally killed numerous prisoners with his gun or his whip. And he conducted his own unique experiments. Mengele gathered hundreds of sets of twins from the tens of thousands of victims at Auschwitz. He measured every part of their bodies, studied their blood, and dissected their corpses. His goal was to discover the secret for producing more and more babies for the Aryan race.

One of the more grisly examples of the blatant exploitation of human suffering for frivolous, sordid pleasure comes from Buchenwald. At the request of the wife of the camp commandant, the skins of prisoners were made into lampshades and other decorative household articles. Tattooed skin was especially desirable for this purpose.[22]

Resistance

Some of the concentration camp internees resigned themselves to an ignoble death, but many resisted. To resist was to risk torture and death, but torture and death would come sooner or later anyway.

They resisted by fighting back. Men and women and teenagers struck out at their tormenters with nothing but their fists and feet and teeth. A woman arriving at Auschwitz plunged the high heel of her shoe into an SS officer's forehead, snatched his gun, and shot two other Nazis.[23]

A prisoner who has been subjected to low pressure experimentation. For the benefit of the Luftwaffe, air pressures were created comparable to those found at 15,000 meters in altitude in an effort to determine how high German pilots could fly and survive. Josef Mengele (inset), a German physician, conducted some of the cruelest experiments.

They resisted by defying orders. They took forbidden notes from one camp to another, stole small comforts from storage rooms and kitchens, exchanged places on work details so that family members could be together. They recited Jewish prayers aloud. They hid pregnant women and newborn babies from certain death for as long as possible.[24]

Those who had some influence resisted by trickery. One prisoner/doctor in Gusen, a satellite of Mauthausen, exaggerated the severity of a minor infection in a *kapo's* finger and amputated his right arm—the arm that wielded the club and the whip.[25]

They resisted by sabotaging their forced work assignments. Men building warplanes dropped pieces of metal into the machinery, stopping the production line.[26] Prisoners steering railcars carrying coal to the crematoriums drove them off their tracks. Unexplained fires brought assembly lines to a halt. Army uniforms that came from prisoner shops had sleeves sewn closed and zippers that did not work. Shoes had soles that came off when water touched the glue. Only one fourth of the guns made at Buchenwald worked, and fewer than half the rockets from Dora-Mittelbau were functional. Inmate laborers intentionally sabotaged whatever items they manufactured: tank engines at Dachau, munitions and spare parts at Ravensbrück, warplanes at Sachsenhausen, and U-boats at Neuengamme.[27]

They resisted by merely staying alive in these places meant for their death. The acts of defiance were small and, in the long run, of little significance. But defiance gave those who had been stripped of everything, including their identity, a measure, however slight, of power over their own lives. These acts permitted those who had been robbed of their humanity to die with dignity.

6

The End of the Camps

Germany was losing the war. In 1943, Russian troops were gaining ground in the east and American and British armies were gaining in the west. Several German cities had been bombed and lay in rubble. The possibility of defeat raised major questions for Hitler about conflicting purposes. The führer had hoped to accomplish two things. He wanted to win the war—to restore national honor, to gain living space for the German people, to extend the flag of the Third Reich over all of Europe. And he wanted to exterminate the Jewish race. He had declared time and again that the outcome of the war would be the annihilation of either the Aryan or the Jew. If he was going to purge Europe of the Jews, he was going to have to do it before the war ended.

Winning the war required turning every hand in the land to the manufacture of armaments—the hands of men and women in Germany, of foreigners in the conquered territories, of prisoners in the concentration camps. But continued extermination of the Jews would wipe out a large number of laborers needed for war production. Army officers argued that the war effort should have top priority and Jews could contribute. They complained that the shortage of labor was devastating the already crippled military. The SS countered that its project—the final solution—was of prime importance.

In the end, Hitler's maniacal anti-Semitism prevailed. The only war industries still permitted to use Jewish labor were those located in or in connection with concentration camps. And those workers were kept alive only because the gas chambers were at full capacity with Jews classified as too weak, too young, or too old to work. The directive from the Reich minister in charge of the occupied territories was clear: "As a matter of principle, economic considerations should be overlooked in the solution of the problem."[1]

Removing the Evidence

The advance of the enemy presented Hitler with a second dilemma. What if the war should be lost, the liquidation of the Jews not be completed, and the world discover what had really gone on in the death camps? The nations that had treated Germany so harshly after World War I were not likely to be kind if they uncovered the terrible secrets of Treblinka or Auschwitz. The crematoriums were destroying evidence day and night, but they could not keep up with the massive piles of corpses, much less with the living dead crowded in the barracks.

Part of the problem was solved by the creation of a new unit of inmates with branches at several camps: Special Commando 1005. The job of Unit 1005 was to open up all the mass graves, burn the corpses buried in them, and scatter the ashes. The first Unit 1005 began its work at Chelmno. Others toiled in forests throughout Poland and western Russia. In the course of almost two years, from mid-1943 to the war's end in April 1945, the remains of more than 2 million people were obliterated.[2]

As the Russian Army pushed the German tanks farther and farther back, the death camps were increasingly in danger of discovery. The first two, Chelmno and Belzec, were already out of commission. Their mobile vans had been far less efficient than the permanent gas chambers, and frequent equipment breakdowns had meant long delays in the deportation schedules. So Belzec had been shut down in November 1942 and Chelmno had been blown up in April 1943. (A year later, Chelmno was reopened to liquidate ten thousand Jews of the ghetto of Lodz but abandoned four months later when the task was completed.)

Treblinka Uprising

As the rumors of Russian advances filtered into the camps, the inmates grew restless. When the processing of people through the death camps slowed, the prisoners who remained alive—mostly the men of the *Sonderkommandos*—sensed that their usefulness to their captors was coming to an end. The possibility of liberation was not nearly as strong as the certainty that the SS would leave no witnesses to their deeds. Several prisoner revolts were spurred by a mix of hope and desperation. They were all brutally crushed, but they did hasten the closing of some camps.

At Treblinka, about one hundred internees formulated a plan, not merely for escape, but for takeover and destruction of the camp. A number of the Polish block leaders and foremen agreed to participate; they knew the Nazis would not spare them when the camp was closed. The attack was carefully and precisely plotted. Weapons would be available because a prisoner locksmith had worked for several months making a key to the camp arsenal, where rifles and grenades were stored. Each person in the growing conspiracy had a specific assignment. Some were to shoot the sentries in the watchtowers, others to overpower the guards in the camp. Some were to cut the telephone lines, others the wire fences. Some were to set certain buildings on fire. Timing was important: at 4:30 in the afternoon the guards would be tired and inattentive. The prisoners would have enough daylight to carry out their revolt and the cover of darkness for their escape. It was crucial that everyone act at once, catching the guards totally by surprise. The signal to begin would be a single rifle shot.

After postponing the attack a number of times, the date was finally set for August 2, 1943. The *kapo* who distributed tools to the work details handed out extra axes for those assigned to cut tree stumps, plus extra wire cutters, pliers, hammers, and knives. Two young prisoners slipped into the arsenal and handed pistols, rifles, and hand grenades through a window to inmates in the construction work detail. The weapons were covered with rags and carried on a stretcher and in buckets to the center of the camp and hidden under piles of potatoes. Gradually, the weapons began to make their way into the hands of the conspirators. By 4:30 P.M., every gun would be in the right hands and everyone would be in place.

Each of the conspirators had hidden away some money to be used when they were out of the camp— money taken from the clothing of those who had perished in the gas chambers. One prisoner ran across the camp and accidentally dropped a gold coin. Possessing anything of value was a crime punishable by

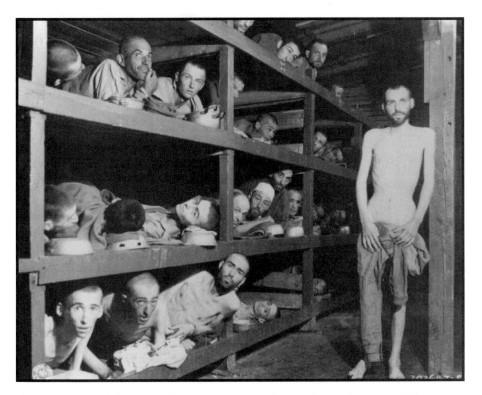

Pictured here are slave laborers in the Buchenwald camp. The prisoners lived in deplorable conditions, often using soup bowls as pillows. Many of the prisoners died of malnutrition.

death. An SS guard dragged the offending inmate to the place of execution.

When the guard's shot rang out in the tenseness of the camp prepared for revolt, stunned inmates wondered what to do. The signal came a half hour too soon. Many weapons still lay under potatoes. Everyone was not in place. The phone lines were not yet cut, and all the inmates were not yet informed. But all had heard what they thought was the signal, and so the revolt began.[3]

Because the precise plans that had been so carefully detailed could not be carried out, the uprising succeeded in saving only a few. Of the eight hundred who tried to escape, about four hundred were killed in the camp. Three hundred more were hunted down by the SS and shot before they could reach safety. About one hundred escaped, but only forty survived the war.[4]

The revolt had destroyed much of the camp. In November, the Nazis blew up what was left of Treblinka, completely leveled the entire site, and planted trees to cover the blood and the ashes.

One observer, however, visiting the area in 1959, fourteen years after Germany's surrender, came across a massive clearing in a thick forest. He noticed that the soil was not brown, but gray. As he felt the dirt trickle through his fingers, he realized that the earth "was coarse and sharp: filled with the fragments of human bone."[5]

Sobibór Uprising

At Sobibór, a very similar revolt took place two months later under the leadership of a Russian Jewish army officer, Sasha Pechersky. It was scheduled for October 14, 1943, at 4:00 P.M. The female prisoners who worked in the SS quarters had stolen pistols, hand grenades, a rifle, and a submachine gun.[6] These weapons, along with knives and hatchets, were smuggled to the thirty men involved in the plot. Then, at 3:30 P.M., the conspirators enticed the camp officers to come to the workshops, one at a time, to be fitted for boots and coats and other clothing. As each officer entered, he was killed by two inmates. Meanwhile, others severed the telephone lines and the electric wires in three of the barbed-wire fences.

Just before 4:00 P.M., the bugle signaled time for roll call. One SS officer had not been located, but the operation was already in motion. As the prisoners assembled on the *Appellplatz*, the conspirators joined them there, dressed in the uniforms of the fallen men. They began to pass word of the plan along the lines. Everyone was to march to the main gate at the cry of "Hurrah." The few weapons the conspirators held would take care of the leaderless Ukrainian guards in the watchtowers.

But as the signal for attack was given, the missing SS officer appeared and began ordering the Ukrainians to open fire. Of the six hundred Jewish prisoners in the camp, all but about fifty sickly ones charged toward the gate.[7] Three hundred escaped, but two hundred of those were killed by the mines hidden just beyond the fence or by the guards scouring the forest for survivors. Perhaps a hundred got away, but many of them were later murdered by anti-Semitic Poles. Only fifty-eight were known to be alive when the war ended.[8] However, this uprising can be considered a victory for the Jewish prisoners since 90 percent of the Nazis at Sobibór were killed.

Sobibór, like Treblinka, was shut down soon after the uprising. In December, the camp was demolished and crops planted to mask all trace of the deaths that had occurred there.

Closing of Other Camps

As these and smaller revolts shook the Nazi leaders, the Russian Army continued to advance. Hitler realized that he would soon need to dismantle the camps in the enemy's path and remove any evidence of their existence. He also was determined to annihilate the Jews while he still had the cover of war. He called the extermination of the Jewish race "a page of glory in our history"—a page that, because the rest of the world would not understand or approve and he could "never speak of it publicly," had "never been written and is never to be written."[9] So the nearness of the Russian Army resulted in an increase in the feverish pace of Jewish extermination in all the labor camps.

At Majdanek, so many Jewish workers were killed that five of the subsidiary camps had to be permanently closed due to a lack of laborers. On a single day, November 3, 1943, SS and policemen from miles around descended with their machine guns on the camp and its satellites. Russian prisoners of war were made to dig huge pits and Jews were lined up at their edges. In the operation code-named Harvest Festival, eighteen thousand to forty thousand people were massacred— every Jew in the camp. The crematoriums were busy day and night, and "a light dust lay over the whole town of Lublin and permeated the air like smoke."[10]

In the spring of 1944, the Russian Army was dangerously close. In order to prevent the workers and the camps from falling into enemy hands, the easternmost camps were evacuated to sites in Germany. More than sixty new camps were set up at Stutthof on the Baltic Sea to receive some of the displaced prisoners. From March through November, primarily non-Jewish inmates were sent west to continue their labor for the Reich while Jews were still being rounded up in France, Holland, Hungary, and Greece and sent to the gas chambers of Auschwitz. There the furnaces continued to blaze until evacuation was finally ordered on January 18, 1945, with the Russian Army only eight days away.

In a few instances, the retreating inmates were transported in trains. More commonly, they went on foot. The twelve-hour-per-day treks—for severely weakened prisoners with little food, inadequate clothing, and skittish guards—amounted to death marches. One survivor recalled receiving a handful of grain to last the four days of the journey from Flossenbürg to Dachau.[11]

94

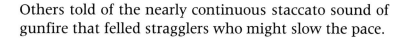

Others told of the nearly continuous staccato sound of gunfire that felled stragglers who might slow the pace.

Liberation

At Majdanek, the SS failed to evacuate all the prisoners and destroy the camp. A group of Polish internees led an attack in which the last six thousand inmates overpowered and captured the guards and the *kapos* and held them until the Russians entered the camp on July 24, 1944.

What the Russians found in Majdanek, the first concentration camp to be liberated, stunned the world. About one thousand emaciated men clung to life amid disease and filth. The six gas chambers were unmistakable; 535 drums of Zyklon B and a number of containers of carbon monoxide gas were located nearby. The function of the crematorium was obvious: human bones could be seen near the five furnaces.

At Auschwitz, also, the final evacuation came too late for all incriminating evidence and all witnesses of mass murder to be destroyed. The thirty satellite camps produced enough arms, synthetic oil and rubber, and other war-related products that Himmler hesitated to abandon what had become one of the largest weapons factories for the Reich. So at Auschwitz, the slave labor, the gassing of Jews, and the SS brutality continued at a frantic pace even as Russian troops expelled German soldiers from nearby cities.

But the Jews of the *Sonderkommando* knew the end was coming. Their only hope of survival, slim as it was, lay in revolt. They enlisted the help of Rosa Robota, a young Jewish woman internee. From some of the girls who labored in the camp ammunition factory, Rosa obtained explosives, which she smuggled to the men. The ambitious plan, like the desperate uprisings in so many other camps, fell far short of victory. One of the

four giant crematoriums was set ablaze and utterly destroyed on October 7, 1944, but the others were spared and all the conspirators but one caught and executed. When Rosa's part in the plot was discovered, she was tortured and hanged alongside three of the female factory workers.[12]

The last gassing at Auschwitz took place on November 28, and the gas chambers were dismantled and shipped to the Gross-Rosen camp in Germany, 150 miles away. Finally, the last sixty-four thousand inmates were ordered out of all the Auschwitz camps on January 18, 1945, and two days later the remaining furnaces were blown up.[13] The prisoners traveled through the snow in their thin prison garb, some in open railcars and many more on foot, to the dozens of camps still open in Germany. For most, the monthlong march covered more than four hundred miles.

On January 27, when Russian soldiers entered Auschwitz, they found 648 inmates dead[14] and 2,819[15] barely alive in its three main camps.

By early 1945, Russian troops were advancing rapidly from the east and the armies of the United States and Great Britain were approaching from the west. Only a narrow band of Germany was still under Nazi control, and the prisoners who survived the death marches were crowded into the camps located there. The terrible debate over whether to use the labor of the

Survivors in Ebensee (top) after being liberated by the U.S. Army. Survivors (middle) suffering from malnutrition and a variety of other diseases in a section of the hospital barracks. The patients in the upper bunks were too weak to go to the latrine, making sanitation conditions intolerable and immediate evacuation necessary. Prisoners in Dachau (bottom) cheer the arrival of American liberators.

inmates to prolong the war or to eliminate the witnesses of mass murders still raged. Himmler tried to accomplish both. He set the prisoners to work repairing roads, rail tracks, bridges, and airfields until the guns of the liberators could be heard. Then as many as could be were killed and the rest marched to camps farther from the battlefront.

But the Allies—Russia, Great Britain, France, and the United States—were closing in more quickly than the SS could retreat. After Auschwitz, the other camps quickly fell into Allied hands. The Western nations reeled from the gruesome revelations. At Ohrdruf, American liberators uncovered several mass graves on April 4, 1945. At Buchenwald, on April 11, U.S. soldiers found cartloads of corpses and a room full of lampshades made of human skin. At Bergen-Belsen on April 15, the British discovered more than ten thousand unburied bodies, victims of a typhus epidemic and starvation. On the same day, the living and the dead were found side by side in the same filthy beds at Nordhausen. At Gardelegen, American troops stared at an open pit in which the logs of a cremation pyre were still burning.

Even the long-hoped-for liberation was, like every other experience in the camps, an occasion of fear and dread for the inmates. At Dachau, the inmates knew

Joseph Schleifstein, a young survivor of Buchenwald, was born in the Sandomierz ghetto in 1941. His parents, Israel and Esther, worked in a slave labor camp near the ghetto but managed to hide Joseph. In 1943, the Schleifsteins were deported to Buchenwald. Joseph's father put him in a large sack, and with the help of the Communist underground in Buchenwald, kept him hidden until the liberation. In 1947, they immigrated to the United States.

something was happening. In the first four months of 1945, 30,358 new arrivals swelled their ranks.[16] The number of selections increased. On Wednesday, April 25, all the labor details housed outside the camp were called in early and the gates locked. On Thursday, seven thousand prisoners were ordered to march south; thirty-two thousand were left.[17] Whispers raced through the camp of tanks just outside the city, of parachutes nearby, of German surrender, and of SS plans to liquidate any survivors. For three days, guards paced and inmates watched in eager silence. Then, on

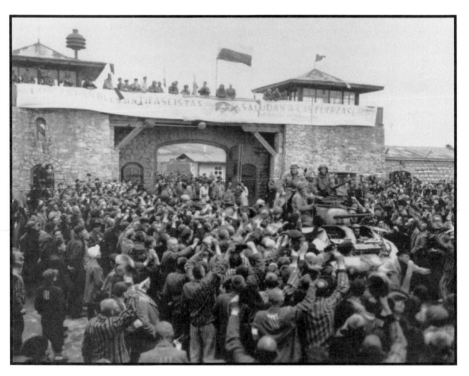

Mauthausen survivors cheer the soldiers of the Second Armored Division of the U.S. Third Army two days after their liberation. Mauthausen, which had the harshest conditions, was the last camp to be liberated. The banner reads: "The Spanish Anti-Fascists Salute the Liberating Forces."

Sunday, April 29, just after noon, a soldier appeared outside the fence. The cry "Americans!" was raised in several languages, and a prisoner darted toward the gate. A guard shot the first internee to welcome the U.S. Army, but others poured after him, and the men in the watchtowers lowered their guns. Disbelieving skeletons lined the fences and cheered. They waved flags of some of the twenty-seven different countries from which they had come, flags they had made from scraps of cloth and somehow hidden, longing for this day. An American army chaplain took the loudspeaker and tearfully invited the now free men to pray. They clasped hands with their fellow sufferers, bowed their heads, and thanked God and America.[18]

The next day—the day Hitler committed suicide—Russia liberated Ravensbrück. One camp remained: Mauthausen, the facility regarded even by the SS as the most severe, the most savage of all.[19] This was the camp where the commandant bragged that he had given his son a birthday present of fifty Jews "as target practice."[20] This was the place to which all the surviving inmates eventually came. This was the place where, despite the fact that military defeat was virtually certain, the commandant ordered a death march south to the satellite Ebensee. There he tried to force thirty thousand men into a tunnel he was prepared to blow up. But the prisoners, emboldened by the nearness of their liberators, refused. When the Americans entered the group of camps from May 5 to May 8, the commandant tried to disguise himself in a striped prisoner uniform. But the inmates knew his hated face well and he was shot and killed.

The same day the last concentration camp was liberated, on May 8, 1945, the Allies accepted Germany's unconditional surrender. The twelve-year reign of the Third Reich was finally over.

7

Never Again

Liberation of the camps did not end the dying. Thousands of people who had been starved, beaten, and worked to exhaustion died within their first week of freedom. For many, their bodies simply gave out. For many others, the rich food the rescuers thought would nourish them to strength was more than their deprived systems could handle. In Dachau, the daily death rate in the days following liberation was two hundred;[1] in Belsen, it was three hundred.[2] But each day the situation improved. Doctors and nurses of the Red Cross international relief organization and of the victorious armies restored two hundred thousand to health.

For some of the former camp inmates, liberation brought new sorrows. They had lost whole families, entire communities. Their homes were destroyed in the war or occupied by people who still hated them simply because they were Jews. Their money, their businesses, and their possessions were all gone. Many were physically and psychologically unable to return immediately to a normal life. For these thousands, three camps were transformed into displaced persons (DP) camps: Bergen-Belsen and Dachau in Germany and Mauthausen in Austria. The barracks that had smelled of burning flesh were cleaned and furnished to provide shelter for those who had nowhere to go.

But still the torment did not end. The camps and other DP centers were not built for comfort, and they did little more than keep the survivors barely alive. Many had no heat, no place to cook, inadequate facilities for washing and bathing. Some were staffed at first by former Nazis, who treated the displaced Jews harshly. Residents fortunate enough to have families had to string ropes across the barracks and hang blankets over them for privacy. Each person was given one set of clothing per year. Food was in short supply and consisted mostly of bread and potatoes. The centers became desperately overcrowded with new waves of Jews fleeing persecution in Poland, Czechoslovakia, Hungary, Romania, and the Soviet Union. By the end of 1946, 204,000 Jews were huddled together in the DP camps of Germany and Austria.[3]

For months after the war ended, refugees poured into the camps by the thousands, but in the months and years that followed, they trickled out at a very slow pace. England had promised the Jews a homeland in Palestine but had limited the number of people who could move there to seventy-five thousand over a five-year period. The United States had set a quota on immigration from Eastern Europe of fifteen hundred people a month, and other countries accepted even fewer. Thus, many remained in DP camps for ten or more years.[4]

As the victims began to pick up the broken pieces of their lives, stories of Nazi cruelty flooded the Western press. The revelations of the torture and murder of civilians ignited a passion in the Allied countries for justice.

Trials

Justice came in the form of war-crimes trials. A number of trials were held, but the most public attempt to force the Nazis to pay for their horrendous deeds began in the Palace of Justice in Nuremberg, Germany, on November 20, 1945. An international military tribunal composed of judges from the Allied nations—the United States, Great Britain, France, and Russia—listened to testimony for almost a year. Twenty-two of the highest ranking members of the Nazi party were accused of crimes against humanity. (One of the twenty-two hanged himself in his prison cell before the trial began.)

As this and other trials proceeded, the entire world was shocked to learn not only of the nature and magnitude of the deeds that were committed, but also of the callous attitude toward the most savage treatment of human beings. The most common defense was "Just following orders." The judges did not accept the attempt to deny personal responsibility by placing all blame on superiors. They found nineteen of the twenty-two guilty and sentenced four to relatively short prison terms, three to life imprisonment, and twelve to death.

The Nuremberg trials ended October 1, 1946, on the Jewish holy day of Yom Kippur, the Day of Atonement. Fifteen days later, the death sentences were carried out.

Fates of Some Nazis

All of the hundreds of men who were guilty of inhuman acts against their fellow man were not brought to justice. Some escaped and were able to

After liberation, many of the prisoners were vengeful and wanted the Nazis to be punished for their acts. A Russian survivor, liberated by the 3rd Armored Division of the U.S. First Army, identifies a former camp guard who brutally beat prisoners.

disguise themselves for years. But a network of concentration camp survivors dedicated themselves to hunting down their tormentors, exposing their barbarity, and seeing them punished, no matter how long the quest might take. Some of the better-known criminals associated with the concentration camps received swift punishment, some eluded capture for years, and some escaped justice altogether.

Reinhard Heydrich, chief of security for the Reich, was assassinated in the middle of the war by Czechoslovakians and died in June 1942. The Nazis retaliated by completely destroying the entire Czech village of Lidice, killing all the males and sending the women and children to concentration camps.

Theodor Eicke, who developed the concentration camp system at Dachau, was also killed before the war ended. After Hitler's invasion of Poland, Eicke left Dachau for the battlefield, taking most of his Death's Head units with him. He was killed in action in Russia in 1943.

Sigmund Rascher, the doctor who conducted medical experiments at Dachau, fell out of favor with Himmler. In February 1945, Himmler had him executed.

Heinrich Himmler, head of the SS, the Gestapo, and the concentration camp system, was captured by the British shortly after Germany's surrender. He had shaved his moustache and disguised himself in the uniform of an army private, with a patch over his eye. Rather than face the justice of his captors, Himmler bit into a capsule of cyanide on May 23, 1945, and was dead twelve minutes later.

Josef Kramer, commandant of Bergen-Belsen, was known as the Beast of Belsen because of the atrocities he committed there. He was condemned by a British court on November 11, 1945, and was executed.

Rudolf Höss, commandant of Auschwitz, was sentenced to death by a Polish court at a trial in Warsaw and was hanged at Auschwitz in the spring of 1947.

Oswald Pohl, head of the SS Economic Administration, was responsible for squeezing the most money for the Reich out of concentration camp labor and the personal effects of the prisoners. He was sentenced to death by the United States Military Tribunal at a 1947 trial in Nuremberg and was executed in 1951.

Adolf Eichmann, chief of the SS Department of Jewish Affairs, was arrested immediately after the war but escaped. He was tirelessly hunted by Israel's secret service and found in 1960, hiding in Argentina. He was kidnapped and brought to trial in Israel. In December 1961, he was condemned to death, and in May 1962 he was executed.

Josef Mengele, the doctor of Auschwitz, escaped after the war ended. He lived in several South American countries—Argentina, Brazil, and Paraguay—under an assumed name. He died in a swimming accident in 1979, but his body was not identified until 1985.

Klaus Barbie, head of the Gestapo in Lyons, France, was so cruel to the Jews he had murdered there or deported to camps in Poland that he was called the Butcher of Lyons. He managed to escape and became active in the Nazi underground, printing false identification papers for himself and other SS officers. Unaware that he was considered a war criminal by the French, the American Counter Intelligence Corps employed him from 1947 to 1951 as a counterespionage agent, supplying information about former Nazis. When Barbie's status as a war criminal became undeniably clear, the United States, in embarrassment over its protection of Barbie, helped him find safe passage to Bolivia in South America. He was found in 1972 by Nazi hunters Serge and Beate Klarsfeld. The Klarsfelds worked for eleven years to have him arrested and brought to trial in France.[5] He was sentenced in 1987 to life imprisonment, and he died in prison.

Preserving the Memory

In addition to seeing their captors punished for their deeds, many of the concentration camp survivors vowed to ensure that the brutality they had suffered

Some concentration camps have been turned into museums and opened to the public. They serve as reminders of this horrifying event. The monument at the entrance to Dachau Memorial Museum reads "Never Again" in four languages—French, English, German, and Russian.

would never be forgotten. They wrote their stories so that the world would know the depths of depravity to which men can sink. They held commemorative ceremonies to honor those who had died and to encourage those who still lived. They built monuments and memorials so that future generations would not repeat the unthinkable madness they had endured.

At Dachau, a committee of survivors determined in 1955 that this first camp would be preserved as a warning to future generations. The barracks were badly deteriorated and had to be torn down, but two were reconstructed. The crematorium was still intact, as was a gas chamber that had been installed late in the war but was never used. The guard towers still stood, and the once electrified wire still surrounded the grounds. The committee collected clothing, records, photographs, and other items so that the world could not deny what had taken place in this and other camps. In 1965, the Dachau Memorial Museum opened.

At the entrance to the museum is a sign that expresses the committee's reason for maintaining this bleak memorial. In four languages—French, English, German, and Russian—are the words "Never Again." Never again, the survivors hoped, should one people be allowed to seek the utter destruction of another. Never again should racial discrimination be made national law in any country. Never again should the world permit a powerful government to torture and kill its citizens. Never again.

Chronology

January 30, 1933
Hitler becomes chancellor of Germany.

March 22, 1933
Dachau, the first concentration camp, is opened.

March 23, 1933
Enabling Act is passed, giving Hitler absolute power.

September 15, 1935
First of the Nuremberg Laws is published, taking rights away from Jews.

August 1936
Concentration camp Sachsenhausen is opened in Germany.

July 1937
Concentration camp Buchenwald is opened in Germany.

March 1938
Germany annexes Austria.

May 1938
Flossenbürg concentration camp is opened in Germany.

August 1938
Mauthausen concentration camp is opened in Austria.

November 9–10, 1938
Kristallnacht: Nazi-instigated rampage against Jewish shops, known as "Crystal Night" or "Night of Broken Glass," ends with the arrest of over thirty thousand Jews.

March 15, 1939
Hitler occupies all of Czechoslovakia.

September 1, 1939
German invasion of Poland begins World War II.

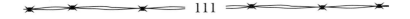

June 14, 1940

Concentration camp Auschwitz is opened in Poland as a prison for Poles and an outstation for colonization of the East.

June 22, 1941

Germany invades Russia.

September 3, 1941

First gassings with Zyklon B at Auschwitz.

Late 1941

Majdanek is opened as a labor camp for Poles and POW camp for Russians.

December 8, 1941

Extermination camp Chelmno is opened in Poland.

January 20, 1942

Wannsee Conference discusses final solution.

Winter 1942 until December 1943

Operation Reinhard undertaken to annihilate all Jews in central Poland.

February 1942

Auschwitz is designated an Operation Reinhard killing center.

March 17, 1942

Extermination camp Belzec is opened in Poland.

May 1942

Extermination camp Sobibór is opened in Poland.

July 23, 1942

Extermination camp Treblinka II is opened in Poland.

November 1942

Belzec is closed.

End of 1942

Gas chambers are installed at Majdanek, making it an extermination camp.

April 1943

Chelmno is destroyed by SS (although it is reopened in 1944 for four months).

August 2, 1943

Revolt at Treblinka; camp is destroyed by SS in November.

October 14, 1943

Revolt at Sobibór; camp is destroyed by SS in December.

November 3, 1943

Operation Harvest Festival: eighteen thousand to forty thousand Jews at Majdanek are massacred.

July 24, 1944

Majdanek, first camp to be liberated, is liberated by Russians.

August 31, 1944

Natzweiler is liberated.

October 7, 1944

Revolt at Auschwitz destroys one crematorium.

November 28, 1944

Last gassings at Auschwitz; camp is ordered to be evacuated on January 18, 1945.

January 27, 1945

Auschwitz is liberated by Russians.

April 4, 1945

Ohrdruf is liberated by the United States.

April 13, 1945

Buchenwald is liberated by the United States.

April 15, 1945

Bergen-Belsen is liberated by British; Nordhausen is liberated by the United States.

Late April 1945

Sachsenhausen is liberated by Russians.

April 29, 1945

Dachau is liberated by the United States.

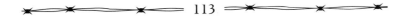

April 30, 1945

Ravensbrück is liberated by Russians; Hitler commits suicide.

May 5–8, 1945

Mauthausen and its satellites, the last remaining camp, is liberated by the United States.

May 8, 1945

Allies accept Germany's unconditional surrender.

November 20, 1945, to October 1, 1946

War criminals are tried at Nuremberg.

Chapter Notes

Chapter 1

1. Adolph Hitler, *Mein Kampf* (Boston: Houghton Mifflin, 1943), p. 59.

2. Lucy S. Dawidowicz, *The War Against the Jews 1933–1945* (New York: Holt, Rinehart and Winston, 1975), p. 17.

3. Barbara Distel and Ruth Jakusch, eds., *Concentration Camp Dachau 1933–1945* (Munich, Germany: Comité International de Dachau, 1978), p. 40.

4. Ibid., p. 20.

5. Dawidowicz, p. 50.

6. Martin Gilbert, *The Macmillan Atlas of the Holocaust* (New York: Macmillan, 1982), p. 15.

7. Nora Levin, *The Holocaust: The Destruction of European Jewry 1933–1945* (New York: Thomas Y. Crowell, 1968), p. 46.

8. Dawidowicz, p. 17.

9. Quoted in Jackson J. Spielvogel, *Western Civilization*, 2nd ed. (Minneapolis/St. Paul: West, 1994), volume II, p. 991.

Chapter 2

1. Barbara Distel and Ruth Jakusch, eds., *Concentration Camp Dachau 1933–1945* (Munich, Germany: Comité International de Dachau, 1978), p. 46.

2. Ibid., p. 42.

3. Ibid., p. 85.

4. Lucy S. Dawidowicz, *The War Against the Jews 1933–1945* (New York: Holt, Rinehart and Winston, 1975), p. 51.

5. Distel and Jakusch, p. 73.

6. Günther Schwarberg, *The Murders at Bullenhuser Damm* (Bloomington: Indiana University Press, 1980), p. 140.

7. Distel and Jakusch, p. 46.

8. Ibid., p. 91.

9. Ibid., p. 94.

Chapter 3

1. Arno J. Mayer, *Why Did the Heavens Not Darken? The "Final Solution" in History* (New York: Pantheon, 1988), p. 333.

2. Ibid., p. 298.

3. William L. Shirer, *The Rise and Fall of the Third Reich: A History of Nazi Germany* (New York: Simon and Schuster, 1959), p. 1249.

4. Gerald Reitlinger, *The Final Solution: The Attempt to Exterminate the Jews of Europe*, 2nd rev. and expanded ed. (New York: Thomas Yoseloff, 1961), p. 102.

5. Brewster Chamberlin and Marcia Feldman, eds., *The Liberation of the Nazi Concentration Camps: Eyewitness Accounts of the Liberators* (Washington, D.C.: United States Holocaust Memorial Council, 1987), p. 30.

6. Shirer, p. 1235.

7. Ibid., p. 1237.

8. Martin Gilbert, *The Macmillan Atlas of the Holocaust* (New York: Macmillan, 1982), p. 35.

9. Barbara Distel and Ruth Jakusch, eds., *Concentration Camp Dachau 1933–1945* (Munich, Germany: Comité International de Dachau, 1978), p. 128.

10. Gilbert, pp. 34–35.

11. Jack Eisner, *The Survivor* (New York: William Morrow, 1980), p. 219.

12. Chamberlin and Feldman, p. 44.

13. Shirer, p. 1238.

14. Ibid., p. 1245.

15. William W. Quinn, comp., *Dachau* (unpublished reports compiled and distributed by 7th U.S. Army), p. 31.

16. Ibid.

17. Shirer, p. 1235.

18. Eisner, pp. 249–250.

Chapter 4

1. Gerald Reitlinger, *The Final Solution: The Attempt to Exterminate the Jews of Europe*, 2nd rev. and expanded ed. (New York: Thomas Yoseloff, 1961), p. 136.

2. Robert Jay Lifton, *The Nazi Doctors: Medical Killing and the Psychology of Genocide* (New York: Basic Books, 1986), p. 136.

3. Ibid., p. 135.

4. Ibid., pp. 139–140.

5. Martin Gilbert, *The Macmillan Atlas of the Holocaust* (New York: Macmillan, 1982), p. 83.

6. Reitlinger, p. 147.

7. Arno J. Mayer, *Why Did the Heavens Not Darken? The "Final Solution" in History* (New York: Pantheon, 1988), p. 392.

8. Lucy S. Dawidowicz, *The War Against the Jews 1933–1945* (New York: Holt, Rinehart and Winston, 1975), p. 149.

9. Reitlinger, p. 148.

10. Ibid., p. 362.

11. Ibid., p. 149.

12. Dawidowicz, p. 149.

13. Reitlinger, p. 113.

14. Ibid., p. 341.

15. Lifton, p. 150.

16. Barbara Distel and Ruth Jakusch, eds., *Concentration Camp Dachau 1933–1945* (Munich, Germany: Comité International de Dachau, 1978), p. 137.

Chapter 5

1. William W. Quinn, comp., *Dachau* (unpublished reports compiled and distributed by 7th U.S. Army), pp. 19–21.

2. Gerald Reitlinger, *The Final Solution: The Attempt to Exterminate the Jews of Europe*, 2nd rev. and expanded ed. (New York: Thomas Yoseloff, 1961), p. 112.

3. Barbara Distel and Ruth Jakusch, eds., *Concentration Camp Dachau 1933–1945* (Munich, Germany: Comité International de Dachau, 1978), p. 71.

4. Quinn, p. 31.

5. Jack Eisner, *The Survivor* (New York: William Morrow, 1980), p. 268.

6. Albert Haas, *The Doctor and the Damned* (New York: St. Martin's Press, 1984), p. 170.

7. Ibid., p. 275.

8. Ibid., pp. 115–119.

9. Albert H. Friedlander, *Out of the Whirlwind: A Reader of Holocaust Literature* (Garden City, N.Y.: Doubleday, 1968), p. 17.

10. Haas, pp. 170–171.

11. Eisner, pp. 247–248.

12. Haas, p. 183.

13. Robert Jay Lifton, *The Nazi Doctors: Medical Killing and the Psychology of Genocide* (New York: Basic Books, 1986), p. 183.

14. Günther Schwarberg, *The Murders at Bullenhuser Damm* (Bloomington: Indiana University Press, 1980), p. 114.

15. William L. Shirer, *The Rise and Fall of the Third Reich: A History of Nazi Germany* (New York: Simon and Schuster, 1959), p. 1281.

16. Ibid.

17. Distel and Jakusch, p. 143.

18. Ibid., p. 149.

19. Shirer, p. 1275.

20. Haas, pp. 271–274.

21. Schwarberg's book is the story of this experiment.

22. Shirer, pp. 1279–1280.

23. Martin Gilbert, *The Holocaust: A History of the Jews of Europe During the Second World War* (New York: Holt, Rinehart and Winston, 1985), p. 621.

24. Barbara Rogasky, *Smoke and Ashes: The Story of the Holocaust* (New York: Holiday House, 1988), p. 104.

25. Haas, p. 265.

26. Ibid., p. 184.

27. Rogasky, p. 102.

Chapter 6

1. Lucy S. Dawidowicz, *The War Against the Jews 1933–1945* (New York: Holt, Rinehart and Winston, 1975), p. 144.

2. Martin Gilbert, *The Macmillan Atlas of the Holocaust* (New York: Macmillan, 1982), p. 168.

3. Samuel Willenberg, "I Survived Treblinka: The Memoirs of Samuel Willenberg," *Revolt Amid the Darkness: 1993 Days of Remembrance* (Washington, D.C.: United States Holocaust Memorial Museum, 1993), pp. 229–232.

4. Gerald Reitlinger, *The Final Solution: The Attempt to Exterminate the Jews of Europe*, 2nd rev. and expanded ed. (New York: Thomas Yoseloff, 1961), p. 153.

5. Martin Gilbert, *The Holocaust: A History of the Jews of Europe During the Second World War* (New York: Holt, Rinehart and Winston, 1985), p. 17.

6. Ibid., p. 618.

7. Moshe Bahir, "Revolt in Sobibor," *Revolt Amid the Darkness: 1993 Days of Remembrance* (Washington, D.C.: United States Holocaust Memorial Museum, 1993), p. 229.

8. Reitlinger, p. 153.

9. Speech delivered to SS leaders, October 4, 1943, cited in Reitlinger, pp. 317–318.

10. Reitlinger, p. 319.

11. Jack Eisner, *The Survivor* (New York: William Morrow, 1980), p. 294.

12. Yuri Suhl, "Rosa Robota: Heroine of the Auschwitz Underground," in *They Fought Back* (New York: Crown, 1967), pp. 219–225.

13. Reitlinger, p. 497.

14. Gilbert, *Atlas*, p. 217.

15. Reitlinger, p. 499.

16. Barbara Distel and Ruth Jakusch, eds., *Concentration Camp Dachau 1933–1945* (Munich, Germany: Comité International de Dachau, 1978), p. 435.

17. Ibid., p. 409; William W. Quinn, comp., *Dachau* (unpublished reports compiled and distributed by 7th U.S. Army), pp. 28–29.

18. Quinn, pp. 29–30.

19. *Revolt Amid the Darkness: 1993 Days of Remembrance* (Washington, D.C.: United States Holocaust Memorial Museum, 1993), p. 404.

20. Gilbert, *Atlas*, p. 233.

Chapter 7

1. William W. Quinn, comp., *Dachau* (unpublished reports compiled and distributed by 7th U.S. Army), p. 6.

2. Martin Gilbert, *The Holocaust: A History of the Jews of Europe During the Second World War* (New York: Holt, Rinehart and Winston, 1985), pp. 793–794.

3. Raul Hilberg, *The Destruction of the European Jews* (Chicago: Quadrangle Books, 1961), pp. 730–731.

4. Ibid., pp. 729–736.

5. Brendan Murphy, *The Butcher of Lyons: The Story of Infamous Nazi Klaus Barbie* (New York: Empire, 1983), pp. 221–305.

Glossary

anti-Semitism—Prejudice against Jewish people.

Appellplatz—Large square area of concentration camps where roll calls took place.

asocial—A person in a category of people who were considered by German police to be unfit for civilian society, including Gypsies, vagrants, and homosexuals.

Black Shirt or Black Guard—A member or members of the *Schutzstaffel* (SS).

blitzkrieg (lightning war)—Quick, sudden, surprise military attack, a technique Hitler used successfully a number of times during World War II.

Brown Shirt—A member of the *Sturmabteilung* (SA).

chancellor—One of the two highest offices in the Weimar Republic (the other being president).

displaced person (DP)—An individual who had no home to which to return after World War II.

Einsatzgruppen (action groups)—Mobile units of the police or SS that followed the German Army into conquered territories. At first, they arrested enemies of Germany, but after the German invasion of Russia, the *Einsatzgruppen* killed Jewish civilians and others by the thousands.

euthanasia—The practice of deliberately killing in a relatively painless way a person who is suffering greatly from an incurable condition. The Nazis used the term for the killing of the physically and mentally handicapped and the aged.

führer—National leader; as chancellor and president of Germany, Hitler adopted the title of "führer."

Gestapo—*The Geheime Staatspolizei,* the State Secret Police.

Holocaust—The attempt of the Nazi government of Germany to completely destroy the Jews of Europe during World War II, from 1939 to 1945.

Judenrein (Jew Free)—Term that meant that all Jews had been removed from a particular geographic area either by deportation or extermination.

kapo—A concentration camp inmate who has been given a position of power over other inmates.

Lebensraum (living space)—Land in Poland and Russia that Hitler thought belonged to the German people by right of their supremacy.

Nazi—A member of, or pertaining to, the National Socialist German Workers' party, a political organization based on principles of extreme nationalism, militarization, racism, and totalitarianism.

Reich—The government of Germany. "The Reich" is often used to refer to the country of Germany, especially under Hitler. *The Third Reich* was the government of Germany under Adolf Hitler, 1933–1945.

Schutzstaffel **(SS)** (protection squad)—Originally an elite group that served as Hitler's personal bodyguards, the SS became, under Himmler, a huge military-like organization that provided staff for camp guards, police units, and some fighting detachments.

Sonderkommando (special squad)—Group of Jewish inmates who were forced to remove gold fillings, rings, hair, and other items from murdered (usually gassed) prisoners in the camps and to take the bodies to the crematoriums. The term is also used of special SS or *Einsatzgruppe* detachments.

Storm Troops—Men of the *Sturmabteilung.*

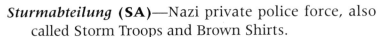

Sturmabteilung **(SA)**—Nazi private police force, also called Storm Troops and Brown Shirts.

synagogue—A Jewish house of worship.

Totenkopfverbände (Death's Heads)—Detachments of soldiers under Theodor Eicke who operated the first concentration camps. They were so named because of the skull and crossbones insignia on their uniforms.

Weimar Republic—The democratic government of Germany between the end of World War I (1918) and Hitler's establishment of the Third Reich in 1933.

→ Further Reading →

Chaikin, Miriam. *A Nightmare in History: The Holocaust, 1933–1945*. New York: Clarion, 1987.

Eisner, Jack. *The Survivor*. New York: William Morrow, 1980.

Forman, James. *The Survivor*. New York: Farrar, Straus, and Giroux, 1976.

Friedman, Ina R. *Escape or Die: True Stories of Young People Who Survived the Holocaust*. Reading, MA: Addison-Wesley, 1982.

———. *The Other Victims: First-Person Stories of Non-Jews Persecuted by the Nazis*. Boston: Houghton Mifflin, 1990.

Oberski, Jona. *Childhood*. Garden City, NY: Doubleday, 1983.

Rogasky, Barbara. *Smoke and Ashes: The Story of the Holocaust*. New York: Holiday House, 1988.

Sender, Ruth Minsky. *The Cage*. New York: Macmillan, 1986.

Spanjaard, Barry. *Don't Fence Me In! An American Teenager in the Holocaust*. Saugus, CA: B and B Publishing, 1981.

Staden, Wendelgard von. *Darkness over the Valley*. New York: Penguin, 1982.

Stadtler, Bea. *The Holocaust: A History of Courage and Resistance*. New York: Behrman House, 1973.

Volavkova, Hana, ed. *I Never Saw Another Butterfly: Children's Drawings and Poems from Terezin Concentration Camp, 1942–1944*. New York: Schocken, 1978.

Wiesel, Elie. *Night*. New York: Noonday Press, 1988.

Index